GW01316110

BECOME A   GOLFER

By PGA Profes... Richard Coffin

This edition published by Richard Coffin Golf, 2017

Copyright © Richard Coffin 2017

All rights reserved. No part of this book may be reproduced in any form or by electronic or mechanical means including information storage and retrieval systems without permission in writing from the publisher except by reviewers who may quote brief passages in their book review.

First edition

Photography by Alan Piper

ISBN: 9781549810268

Published by Richard Coffin Golf, Tiverton, Devon, United Kingdom

Contact the publishers/author: rcoffin@hotmail.co.uk

References: Cochran, A., & Stobbs, J. (1968). The Search for the Perfect Swing. Heinmann

Dedication

My first golf book has to be dedicated to my family.

To my late Dad, for getting me into the game that has punctuated my whole life, and for showing me a good grip which has become the foundation of my playing and teaching. It's a shame that he hasn't seen me become the golf professional that his early encouragement has inspired me to become, but I hope he would have been proud.

To my Mum, for her unwavering love and single-handed support throughout my life, and for ferrying me here, there, and everywhere to golf tournaments and countless other sporting events when I was young.

Finally, and definitely not least, to my beautiful young daughter who has become the inspiration for almost everything I do. Her patience and understanding, whilst I have been endeavouring to finish this book, has been so much appreciated ... and I'm sure will be generously rewarded with a shopping trip or two very soon!

I love you all

Contents

10.3.3 Playing steeply uphill 152

10.3.4 Playing steeply downhill 153

10.3.5 In summary of sloping lies 154

10.4 Water Hazards 155

10.5 Bunkers 155

10.5.1 Playing from a shallow fairway bunker 156

10.5.2 Greenside Bunker Shots 158

10.5.2.1 Beginner level explosion shot 160

10.5.2.2 Intermediate/Expert Level 163

10.5.3 Bunker Shot Summary 165

10.6 Playing in the wind 165

10.6.1 Playing into the wind 168

10.6.2 The Knockdown Shot 169

10.6.3 Playing with the wind 171

10.6.4 Cross-winds 171

10.6.5 Putting in the wind 172

10.7 Playing in wet weather 173

10.8 When it's cold 174

10.9 Awkward lies summary 175

CHAPTER 11 177

Take Your Medicine (Course Management) 177

11.1 What do we mean? 177

11.2 Improve from the hole backwards 177

CHAPTER 1

Introduction:

Throughout this book, I want you to start thinking about your golf in a new way. I want you to stop trying to FIX the faults you believe you have in your golf swing, putting stroke or chipping technique and concentrate on introducing purely GOOD HABITS into your game. To become a better golfer, you should strive to do the things that better golfers do; you should adopt the good habits that are associated with better golf.

Good players do NOT have perfect golf swings. They do NOT hole every putt and they do NOT always hit every target. They DO however have a sufficient number of overriding good habits to compensate for their many (so-called) faults. Yes, even the greatest of players have multiple faults in their swings (some quite alarming ones) but somehow it doesn't stop them playing the kind of golf most of us only dream of.

In the four decades that I have been playing, watching and teaching golf, I have observed that good players, very good players and top players, all have a few fundamental good habits in common. I have also observed that untutored beginners, high handicappers and generally high scoring players, also have many habits in common; usually recurring bad habits that lead to inconsistent and unsatisfactory golf. I have learned, therefore, that good habits far outweigh the bad ones. We all have far too many so-called faults in our swings to fix them all but by adopting a few of the fundamental good habits that all good golfers have we can cover up a multitude of other sins. It is also much easier to teach and learn these good habits than to attempt to correct all the bad ones. We all have bad habits which we don't always recognise or control but it's never too late to adopt the new habits which will help us become better golfers.

In this book, I want to show you that by adopting only a few simple good habits you can become a much better all-round golfer. I want to show you that by copying some of the things that better players do and by thinking in some of the same ways that better players think you too can become that better player.

Whether your goal is to break a hundred, ninety, eighty or even seventy for the first time (and keep doing it) following the simple concepts in this book will help you achieve your goal. Of course, you can't do it by reading alone. You will need to practise. You will need a can-do attitude. Above all, however, you will need to give up your search for the perfect swing ... I want you to use the swing you have but in a more efficient way.

You will also need to be honest enough to accept that your short-game and putting are at least equally complicit in your current performance and it's not just your ability to hit your long shots from the tee, or fairway, which makes you the player you are. The good habits I will show you will undoubtedly improve all areas of your game but a significant proportion of this book is dedicated to putting, chipping and pitching, in the same way, that a significant proportion of your score is made up from these shorter shots.

I believe that many golf swing theorists and many golf coaching books give the impression that the techniques required to play your best golf are complicated and therefore difficult to learn but may only be appropriate if you are that better player already. Most of my teachings are natural and relatively simple to implement.

In my opinion, the golf swing is a completely natural motion that involves swinging a stick, with a modicum of speed and control, allowing the ball to get hit during the process. That's not to say the game itself is easy ... far from it, as the margins for error are enormous, but ironically it seems that the harder we try to control these margins and limit the errors, the worse the results become. We have to learn to 'swing the stick' with conviction and give up over-conscious control.

In this book, I will talk very little about detailed technique (with the exception of the short game where I believe that very simple new habits will transform your chipping and putting), but I will keep emphasising that by adopting and repeating some fundamental good habits, you can transform yourself into a much better golfer.

CHAPTER 2

So, what are these good habits?

2.1 Good habits outweigh bad habits

I will go on to explain in greater detail each of the good habits of the better golfer as briefly outlined in this chapter. These good habits are at the core of my coaching and the core of what I believe separates better players from high scorers. By incorporating even a few of these good habits and sticking with them you will see a rapid improvement in your golf.

The key words here are STICKING WITH THE GOOD HABITS! We are all striving for consistency in this relentlessly difficult game and yet we don't do consistent things. We inevitably try something new almost every week in order to try to fix our so-called faulty swing (a kind of experimental *'stabbing in the dark'* if you like) just hoping that something will fall into place. And quite often it does but it doesn't last long as we tend to try something else after the first bad shot or two we hit. We are therefore nurturing inconsistency by doing inconsistent things ... and we still wonder why our scores are disappointing!

Good players, as already mentioned, do not have perfect swings (some very far from perfect) but they do not think about these imperfections when they play. Admittedly they will try to fix things from time to time, as even better players want to get even better, but they became good players in the first place by letting the good habits outlined in this book become intrinsic to their play. They trust the swings they do have and repeat them to the best of their ability in spite of knowing they are flawed.

If there is a magic secret to golf it's this ... *'repeat the same good habits at the same tempo with the same routine over and over again and you will be consistent'*. This may not give you *'perfect'* golf but at least you'll be consistent and will undoubtedly improve. You will have a good platform upon which you can build an even better game when you soon become that better golfer.

Good habits apply equally to the full swing, putting, short-game, trouble shots, course management and the mental game alike, so I have broken them down into sections allowing you to work on each aspect of your game as required. Here is a brief outline of the good habits which will be expanded upon in subsequent chapters. These chapters are not in order of importance within the book but follow a logical sequence for improvement.

2.2 Equipment

I mention equipment early in this book as it is a widely misunderstood area of the sport. The misapprehension in the early days that 'any clubs will do' or the belief later on that *'snazzy'* new clubs will be your salvation are common misconceptions. This chapter will deal with the basics of matching clubs to YOU in order to maximise your potential at whichever level you currently play. I will emphasise the importance of the correct length for all the clubs in your bag (including your putter). Also, the ideal shaft flex, club-head size and grip size for all your clubs as well as the ideal loft for your driver and wedges. This chapter could save you hundreds of Pounds, Dollars, Euros or Yen, in the futile search for the magic club.

2.3 Grip

How you hold the club will have a major influence on what happens to your golf ball. Your grip has one of the biggest influences over how much club head speed you can muster and therefore how far you can hit the ball. It is also the primary influence over the angle of your club face at impact and therefore how accurately you can hit the ball. Quite simply, better players have better grips. It the simplest good habit to get into if you are prepared to feel a little awkward for a while and the chapter 'how to hold your golf club' explains in detail how a better grip can be achieved.

2.4 Swing; don't hit!

The oldest expression in the book is *'let the club do the work'* ... but what does this really mean? The club clearly isn't going to do it on its own and what do we even mean by the club? This chapter will deal with the most crucial aspect of the swing; that it primarily IS a swing and NOT a hit, swipe, slash or smash at the ball. All good ball-strikers swing the club-head THROUGH the ball and not AT the ball ... and they all finish in the same position at the end of every swing.

2.5 Swish to the finish

If there is one thing that you take from this book and one thing only it should be that a good rhythm and tempo in your golf swing will compensate for a huge number of other so-called faults in your swing. Even a robot built with a mechanically perfect golf swing will not hit the ball straight or as far if its timing is out. The golf ball is in contact with the golf club for between 0.4 and 0.6 of a millisecond (Cochran and Stobbs, 1968) so, even if your swing is perfect (which nobodies is), if your timing is off, the shot will be errant. This chapter will help you achieve a consistent rhythm as a good habit that will underpin everything else you do in all your golf shots from long drive to tap-in putt.

2.6 Hole more putts

Love it, hate it, or can't see the point of it, the challenge of playing better golf cannot avoid the *game within the game*' that is putting. Whilst somewhere between 35% and 45% of your score is made up from putts you cannot afford to view putting as the easy or 'irrelevant' part of the game. If you are averaging more than two putts per green then you are throwing shots away. If you are not getting your first putt within two feet of the hole then you are going to miss a lot of second putts. If you are missing a high proportion of your three to six-foot putts then you need to adopt some better habits to help improve your putting.

2.7 The Magic Triangle

This is a term I came up with to help you visualise the technique for chipping and most of your short-game shots. Essentially it is designed to help you take your hands out of the shot. Your hands can be too active and cause a multitude of bad habits to evolve. This good habit if acquired and practiced will revolutionise your control around the greens.

2.8 See it, feel it, do it (the mental side of golf)

Sounds easy, doesn't it? But we often find ourselves 'seeing', 'feeling' and 'doing' something completely different to that which we should be seeing, feeling and doing. It's all too easy in golf to fear the worst and therefore sometimes see only the negative. The simple strategies in this chapter will help you think more clearly and execute your best shots when it really matters ... out on the golf course. The old clichés of *'staying in the moment'*, *'one shot at a time'* and *'take your medicine'* apply as equally today as they always have!

2.9 Take your medicine

This is a well-known and often used phrase in golf which suggests that, if you get into trouble on the golf course, you don't compound your error by attempting a heroic recovery which is likely to end in more disaster. This chapter also deals with the wider topic of *course management* which requires you to have a plan for your game and a strategy for most situations you may encounter on the course.

2.10 Trouble shots

This chapter deals with the difficult shots that all players will encounter in almost every round that is played. In this section, I will help you improvise your stance and swing so that you can deal more easily with tricky situations such as sloping lies, thick rough, bunkers, trees, windy days and other inclement weather. Being *'in trouble'* is an inevitable part of the game but having the confidence to escape successfully will help your thinking and your score.

2.11 Technical stuff

Understanding ball flights, ball positions, swing paths, clubface angles and a little of *what causes what* will help you to identify what may be wrong with your golf swing. Knowing what your club is doing as it strikes the ball can play a big part in what you do in order to change your ball flight.

2.12 Effective practise

Practising your golf is important but if you don't practise effectively you won't learn very much. Hitting balls on the range is great fun, in itself, but you will need to put some structure around your practise sessions to acquire good habits and most importantly, take them with you to the golf course. This chapter will help you practise in two distinctive ways and put a definite purpose behind each session.

CHAPTER 3

Glossary of terms used throughout this book

Normally, a glossary might go at the back of the book as a reference to the terminology used throughout. This book is, intentionally, as non-technical as possible for such an in-depth sport, but I thought it more appropriate for you to be aware of, and understand, the most common golfing terms as early as possible in the reading process.

Animal scrape	Any damage to the ground caused by a wild animal
Ball Position	Location of ball in relation to the stance. Described as forward (more opposite front foot), or back (more in the middle) of the stance.
Birdie	A one-under par score on any hole
Bogey	A one-over par score on any hole
Borrow	The amount you have to aim away from the hole when putting due to a slope

Bounce	The degree of bulge on the sole of the club
Break	See 'Borrow' above
Chip	Another name for pitch
Closed clubface	Position of the club when the toe is turned in towards you
Closed stance	Your feet and body alignment is to the right of target (for right-hander)
Cup	Golfer's slang for the hole
Dog-leg	A par four or par five with a pronounced bend in the fairway
Draw	A gently curving ball-flight which lands on target. Curves right-to-left for a right-handed player.
Duffed	A very badly mishit shot
Fade	A gently curving ball-flight which lands on target. Curves left-to-right for a right-handed player.
Fat	Striking the ground well before the ball

Feel	Our perception or sense of something intangible
Hanging lie	When the ball is situated below the level of your feet
Hazard	A bunker, lake, pond or ditch designed to trap your ball
Heel	Part of the club-head nearest to you at set-up with the ball
Hook	A significantly curving ball-flight which misses the target to the left (opposite for a left-hander)
Hosel	The rounded stalk section of the club-head where the shaft is joined. Also called the shank
Impact	The moment of contact with the ball
Length	The overall length of a golf club
Lie Angle	The angle the shaft makes with the ground when setting up to the ball
Loft	The amount of upward angle on the clubface

Match-play	A form of golf played head-to-head and hole-by-hole
Offset clubface	When the clubface is manufactured to be set back from the hosel
On-plane	When the golf club is considered to be at the correct angle throughout the swing
Open clubface	The clubface is angled away from you at set-up
Open stance	Your feet and body alignment are to the left of target (for right-hander)
Over-the-plane	When the golf club is considered to be over-the-top or outside of the ideal position in the backswing or approach to the ball
Par	A score on an individual hole or for an entire round equal to the number suggested on the scorecard.
Pin	Golfer's slang for flagstick
Pitch	A short approach shot to the green which does not require a full swing

Pot bunker	A deep, round and relatively small type of sand-trap
Pull	A misdirected ball-flight that flies straight left for a right-handed player
Reading (green)	Surveying the contours of the green prior to putting
Rough	The longer thicker grass bordering the fairways and greens
Sand wedge	A specially designed lofted club for helping an escape from a bunker
Scratch	Golfer's slang for a zero-handicap player
Semi-rough	Slightly longer grass cut between the fairway and thick rough
Shank	A mishit ball that strikes the rounded inside edge of the club's hosel
Slice	A significantly curving ball-flight which misses the target to the right. (opposite for a left-hander)

Stroke	Describes each shot played during a round of golf. Could also describe your putting swing
Stroke-play	Form of golf when every shot is recorded for the hole and marked on a card
Sweet Spot	The absolute centre of gravity of the club-head
Swing centre	Coaching term describing the centre-point of your golf swing. Generally considered to be the top of one's sternum
Swing plane	The inclined angle of your golf swing
Target line	The imaginary line drawn between your ball and its target.
Tee	A small peg that the ball can be balanced on at the start of each hole.
Teeing ground	The area defined by coloured blocks and the starting position for each hole.
Test the surface	Touch the line of your shot with your club or hand (or the sand in a bunker)

Thin	Hitting the ball near to or above its equator
Tight Lie	A ball situated on very closely mown grass or bare hard ground.
Toe	The end of the club-head furthest from you at set-up
Topped	Striking the ball at its very top causing a very short low running ball-flight
Under-the-plane	When the golf club is considered to be lower than or underneath the ideal position in the backswing or approach to the ball.
Up and down	Golfer's slang describing a short approach to the green followed by only one putt.
Waggle	The subtle movement of the wrists and club-head prior to the swing.
Yips	An involuntary twitch of the hands just before impact.

CHAPTER 4

Equipment; Understand it and you could save a lot of hassle ... and money.

4.1 A 'minefield' of jargon and confusion

I mention equipment early in this book as it is important for you to understand the role your equipment plays (or doesn't play) in the game of golf. Beginners may believe that *'any old club'* will do and, of course, don't yet have enough knowledge to distinguish between a good or a bad club. More established players can quickly become drawn into the clever marketing of the big brands in golf club manufacture. This marketing can easily convince you that the latest evolution of their driver will hit the ball further than ever, reduce ball spin off the club face so you'll slice it less, or that their *'revolutionary'* new irons will be more accurate and 'forgiving' than your current model.

In this chapter, I won't blind you with science or dwell on *'maximum moments of inertia'* or *'variable face thicknesses'.* I will, however, explain the basic principles involved in ensuring you have the right clubs for your level of play at different points in your development. I will go through the main components in your set, in order of the most common misconceptions surrounding their value to your game, namely: driver, fairway woods, hybrids, irons, wedges and putter ... rather than their order of importance which, in my opinion, would be the other way around. I will also be brutally honest enough to tell you straight that, provided your clubs are of reasonable quality and are the right size for you, then 100% of what happens to the ball thereafter is (I'm afraid) solely down to you. You will, therefore, gain much more by improving your own golfing habits than you ever will in the search for that elusive game-changing club. It will also save you money if you patiently work on your own game, combined with regular swing checks from your teaching professional, rather than wasting bundles of cash on updating your clubs every year.

It seems that almost every six months there is a new club on the market promising more distance, bigger sweet spots, more adjustability, lower spin rates, higher ball speeds, improved trajectory or a magic shaft material which will launch your ball into outer space. The truth is that all golf club manufacturers have to work within the rules of golf as set out by the R&A and USGA and these are getting stricter rather than eased. There is a limit to what a golf club and golf ball is allowed to do. Golf balls could be made to fly 400 yards for the average player and drivers could be made even bigger with even more space-age technology to send the ball out of sight. The rules, however, restrict these things so that golf courses don't have to be made even longer than they are becoming. With this in mind, you can bet your last pound, bottom dollar or a million rupees that ALL manufacturers are making clubs right at the limit of these rules and these rules haven't changed drastically for a long time. So, as long as your clubs are reasonably modern (i.e. no more than 10 years old), they will be quite capable of allowing you to play some great golf. What is more important, by far, is that you get the basics of club-fitting correct. The basics of club length, lie angle, swing weight, shaft flex, shaft material, appropriate loft, club-head design, set composition (distance gapping), club face angle and grip size are far more fundamental to golf club performance than any fancy marketing 'spin' you may be tempted by!

4.2 The Driver

The *'Big Dog'* in your bag is the club that can be the most fun to hit when you get it right but it can also be the club that gets you into the most trouble; your round can be over even before it starts if you can't keep your ball in play. You are therefore more at the mercy of the marketing men and women who will convince you that a new driver is the answer to your prayers. Most modern drivers have adjustable hosels allowing you to alter the angle of the club face or increase or decrease the loft of the club. The marketing argument is that you can adjust your driver to the optimum setting in order to improve your ball flight or stop you from slicing or hooking so much. In reality, these adjustments make very little difference to the average player, but leaves that player tinkering with the settings and never really playing with the same club twice ... and still they wonder why their tee shots are inconsistent! You probably can't avoid buying a driver which is adjustable these days (as most of them are) but you should, at least, use the right settings for YOU right now ... and stick to it. Constantly tinkering with the settings will only add to inconsistency and more doubt!

4.3 Driver Length

Most men's 'off the shelf' drivers are around 46" long. Using pure physics, the longer the club the more club-head speed can be generated and therefore the further the ball will go. In reality, for a human being, the longer the club the less likely it is that you will hit the sweet spot consistently and the more difficult it is to control the clubface angle at impact with the ball. Even tour pros who are the longest and most consistent drivers in the world recognise the importance of hitting the sweet spot for maximising distance and accuracy. A ball hit down the middle of the fairway also has less far to go to the green for your next shot than a drive that may be longer but has to come into the green from an angle. It, therefore, comes as no surprise that the average length of a men's driver on tour is around 44.5" ... so why should the average golfer be expected to hit a 46" driver better than a tour pro?! I make my drivers for my customers at 43.5 inches for mid to high handicap male golfers and 42.5" for most lady players.

4.4 Driver Loft

The amount of vertical angle (known as loft) on your driver can be your friend or foe. Most golfers play with a driver that has too little loft. The lower the loft on a golf club the more side-spin is created by an across the line impact, therefore, exaggerating the amount of slice or hook on your tee shot. If you slice the ball then you will experience your ball flying too high and weakly off into the rough or worse. You will therefore probably change your driver (or its setting) to a lower loft in an attempt to keep the ball down. This will, however, result in even more bend in your shots and won't change the trajectory very much. The slice is the result of an open clubface at impact and if your clubface is open then you have added many degrees of loft to your driver. Most players would benefit from using a more lofted driver. One of at least eleven degrees and even up to fourteen degrees will help you hit much straighter drives. An offset clubface (see glossary) is one of the few golf club technology features that will help your slice somewhat, but, unfortunately, your slice is caused by your swing and no club (however expensive and fancy it is) can cure a slice on its own.

4.5 Fairway Woods

The same effects of length and loft apply equally to your fairway woods. The longer the club, and the lower the loft, the harder it is to get the ball airborne and the more likely it is to spin offline. A number three wood may be a great alternative to a driver off the tee (and for most golfers may leave a shorter second shot as it is more likely your ball will land on the fairway more often) but is one of the hardest clubs in your set to hit successfully off the ground. Once again loft is your *'friend'* with fairway woods and, as a higher trajectory, and ball carry, are requirements of distance, then most golfers will hit a five wood or even a seven wood further than a three wood from a fairway lie (don't even think about a three wood from the rough unless your ball is sitting right on top of the grass). The length of your fairway woods may vary according to your ball-striking ability, but as a general rule, your three-wood should be an inch to two inches shorter than your driver and your five and seven woods an inch shorter respectively.

It is also important to understand that the number stamped on your fairway woods (3, 4, 5, 6, 7 etc.) may be different from one manufacturer to another. The actual amount of loft measured in degrees is the only important number on the club head. A three wood, for example, can vary between thirteen and sixteen degrees and a five wood could be seventeen or even twenty-one degrees and so on. (NB: If the loft isn't stamped on your clubs your professional can measure it for you).

In summary, you must ensure that all your fairway clubs have progressively more loft as the numbers get higher and the shafts get shorter otherwise you could find that all your woods will go the same distance.

4.6 Hybrids (also known as 'rescues' or utility clubs)

Personally, I don't like the word *'rescue'* when describing these clubs as it gives the impression that you can expect a miraculous recovery shot from anywhere or from any lie. Hybrid is a more accurate term as these clubs are designed to bridge the gap between your fairway woods and your longer irons. You may find, for example, that the longest iron you can strike consistently is a six, or even a seven iron, which will leave a big distance gap between your irons and fairway woods. The more traditional longer irons, the five, four, three and dare we mention a number two iron ... are notoriously difficult to strike cleanly or accurately (especially without the aid of a tee) and the new hybrid clubs have evolved to take their place. The wider sole and hollow club-heads provide more forgiveness on off-centre strikes and usually provide a much more successful alternative for most golfers. Despite these facts of physics, many golfers state that they don't have any more success with these hybrid clubs than they do with their long irons. This is due to players swinging with them as if they are irons when in fact they should be thought of as mini woods.

From an equipment perspective, however, the same thinking should be applied to the hybrid clubs as your fairway woods. Each one should be of a different length and loft in order to notice a sufficient gap in distance between each hybrid club. This theory actually applies to every club in your bag; consequently, I have included more information later in this chapter (and also in chapter 13.7) detailing the ideal set make-up in terms of woods, hybrids irons and wedges for different categories of player. You will, therefore, learn the ideal set composition for your game right now, or what the ideal set of clubs may comprise at the next level of your improvement.

4.7 Irons and Wedges

Second, only to your putter, the irons and wedges in your set are the most important clubs in your bag. Why? ... because they are the clubs you hit most often and are the clubs that you can often rescue your score with after an errant tee shot or miscued fairway wood. These clubs are predominantly struck directly from the ground and therefore the factor of 'lie angle' as well as length and loft becomes important. The lie angle of the club-head dictates the angle your club shaft makes with the ground and therefore where the grip end of the club is in proximity to you. If the shaft angle leans too low to the ground (too flat) then you will have to bend forward too much to reach it and vice versa if the shaft angle is too high (too upright) your hands will be too high. If the lie angle of the iron is wrong for you then the wrong part of the sole of the club could strike the ground first causing the ball to fly offline through no fault of your own. Primarily, the length and lie angle of your irons are deduced from your height and length of your arms. However, other factors such as club-head speed and swing tempo also affect the way the shaft flexes throughout the swing and therefore affects how

Your irons should be manufactured to fit your build and set-up

the sole strikes the ground. You should seek professional advice in order to establish the correct lie angle for your irons.

As far as club-head design is concerned irons vary more than any other club in the bag. The head design that many professional players use has changed very little in the last 30-40 years but the irons that you can buy have developed dramatically during this time. The main two elements of iron club-head design are the size of the head and the amount of extra weight that is distributed around the edges of the club. Very simply put, the bigger the head, and the larger the cavity in the back, the more forgiving the club will be for the less consistent ball striker. A better player who hits the sweet spot most of the time prefers a club head that is more responsive to the vagaries of the strike and therefore provides more feedback to the player (sometimes even negative feedback through your fingers and hands can help to subliminally readjust for a better strike next time).

Having said this, don't get drawn into the battle between the marketing companies who promote the top brands as they will, of course, all say their own brand of clubs is the best. The truth is that all the quality brands make equally good clubs, but the best clubs are the right ones for you right now.

As regards the wedges, the most important thing is to get the distance *'gapping'* right. Therefore, the most relevant factors are length and loft as these (two factors) have the most influence over distance. The lie angle also has an influence and is important, but provided that the lie angle is correct before you swing, the *'dynamic'* lie angle at *impact* will be less affected by the lower swing speed of your shorter clubs (*'dynamic'* referring to the lie angle at impact which changes due to the bending of the shaft during the swing; in this case, the wedge shaft being less affected than, for example, a full swing with a five iron).

A lot is said about *'bounce'* these days but in my opinion, this is over complicating things. Yes, a lower bounce angle (see glossary) will help you on tight lies and a higher bounce angle will help you out of a bunker, but I think most of this talk is centred on the manufacturers trying to sell you more wedges. If you believed everything that was said then you'd have at least twelve wedges in your bag!

4.8 Putters

I mentioned at the beginning of this chapter that, if written in the order of importance for your game, your putter would be at the top of that list. The putter is the club that you use the most often in every round you play and therefore contributes the most to your score. You could argue that many of your putts are only tap-ins and don't really count, but those tap-ins are the result of all the putts you have unfortunately already missed.

You can love putting or you can hate it, but you're far more likely to be successful at it if you choose to love it! That thinking applies equally to your putter. It is very easy to *'fall out of love'* with your putter, but unless it's bent, or the grip is on crooked, or it's completely the wrong length and lie angle for your style, then it really isn't the putter's fault … it's far more likely to be the *'puttee!'* (person putting).

You can spend a small fortune these days on the latest *'virtually impossible to miss with putter'*, but some of the greatest putters of all time putted beautifully with nothing more than a rusty flat bit of metal on the end of a stick (and we're not talking centuries ago here either). However, there are only four things that must happen in putting for your ball to go in the hole (assuming that an imperfect green does not disrupt the roll of the ball)

1. You must have calculated the correct line for the putt (i.e. read the break).
2. The putter face must be square to that line at impact.
3. The putter head must be travelling at the correct speed as you strike the ball.
4. The ball should be struck from the middle of the clubface.

OK, I know it's not that easy in real life, but any undamaged putter of any age and any price is more than capable of these things.

In the chapter offering my opinions on putting set-up and technique, I advocate a comfortable position with your eyes directly over the line of your putt. In order to achieve this, you will need a putter of a specific length depending on your height and length of arms. Most standard putters are too long to achieve this position so it is likely that yours will need shortening (this is an easy and inexpensive thing to do).

After considering the length of your putter it is important that the sole of the putter lies flush with the ground, i.e. without a pronounced gap under the heel end (the end nearest to you) or the toe end (furthest away). Any significant gap of this kind means the putter has the wrong lie-angle for your set-up. By contradiction, many good, and even great putters, putt with the toe way in the air or the putter tipped forward slightly with a gap under the heel, but these are exceptions to the norm.

There are literally thousands of different putter head designs but, essentially, they fall into two distinct categories … mallets and blades. A mallet putter is generally much bigger and is much deeper from the face to the back of the putter enabling a longer target line or even simulated golf balls to be drawn on it. The lie angle is usually a bit more upright allowing you to stand a little nearer to the ball if this works for you and may possibly suit the player that prefers a stroke that is fairly straight back and straight through.

A blade putter used to be just that; a narrow piece of metal attached to a shaft and the kind that virtually every player of the early twentieth century and before would have used. The modern bladed putter has evolved, usually incorporating extra weighting on the toe and heel ends of the putter head. This weighting is designed to resist the twisting of the putter head caused by off-centre strikes and therefore gives a better result from a mishit. Bladed putters are often favoured by players who may prefer a slightly more rounded stroke.

It would be pertinent to mention at this point that there is no right or wrong for the path your putter takes on the backstroke and forward stroke. Some top players try to swing the putter straight back and through and others prefer an arc in the stroke. Either way clearly works and some putters suit one more than the other as indicated above. However, both these strokes still require the putter to be square to the correct line at impact and must be travelling at the appropriate speed for the putt at hand.

So, the overall message here is that you must find a putter you like, is of the correct length for you, and that suits the stroke with which you are comfortable. You must then stick with it and learn to love it ... it's never the putter's fault when you miss! Changing your putter every few months may work for a short time (a kind of placebo effect) but it won't last for long!

4.9 Set composition

The rules of golf dictate that you can only carry fourteen clubs during a round of golf: therefore, deciding which ones you carry is vitally important. There seems to be more variety in clubs with every season that passes. Not so long ago there was no such thing as a hybrid club or a gap wedge; if you believed the marketing people you would need to carry about 25 clubs!

Practically speaking, however, the more clubs you carry the harder it is to decide which one to use at any particular time. I see inexperienced players who carry more than one club designed to do the same job and also seem confused by the numbers on the woods and hybrids, or by the names of the wedges. They may carry a seven wood and a number three hybrid for instance, or other clubs with the same length and loft (but with different descriptions or numbers), that will essentially do the same job and hit the ball the same distance. It is important that each club in your bag, if struck correctly, will hit the ball a different distance. It is, therefore, also vital that you know how far each club in your set goes and for what purpose it's in your bag. If you are not sure of this, it makes sense to take every other club out of your set, as there will then be a more noticeable difference in the distance and trajectory (of ball flight) for each club. As a maxim, always remember that the major influences over distance are the length of the club, the loft of the club and how near the middle of the clubface you strike the ball. The number written on the bottom of the club by the manufacturer means very little without considering the loft of the club or the length of the club in comparison to the clubs around it within your set.

If you are a beginner, you should not carry any more than half a set of clubs. Carrying every other club (maybe odd numbers or even numbers) will make choosing which club to use much easier and also keep the distance gaps between each club more noticeable. A more experienced player may need to choose between carrying a larger selection of wedges or a larger selection of the longer clubs (with only fourteen clubs allowed there needs to be a compromise one way or another). In any scenario, however, you need to be sure that every club in your set is there for a specific reason.

4.10 Shaft material and Flex

Despite all the fashionable and complicated names, the material used to make golf club shafts fall into two main categories: either steel or graphite. However, there are literally thousands of different shafts available and you would need a master's degree in physics to fully understand the claimed differences between them! There are steel shafts available that are lighter and more flexible than graphite shafts and vice versa, but it is usually accepted that steel shafts are generally heavier and less flexible than graphite shafts. Steel shafts are generally for stronger hitters and graphite shafts are more helpful to junior players, ladies and senior men.

A lighter and more flexible shaft, combined with an appropriately weighted club-head, is able to generate more club-head speed for the less powerful player. In fact, virtually all players use graphite shafts in their driver, fairway woods and hybrid clubs, but the stronger player will usually play with a much heavier and less flexible option which offers more control.

Both steel and graphite shafts come in a variety of different flexes and all have slightly differing 'maximum bend points' (sometimes called 'kick-points'). Shaft flexes come in varying degrees of flexibility including extra stiff, stiff, regular, senior, ladies and junior. However, these are very general descriptions and one manufacturer's regular may be another one's senior, or vice-versa. A lot is written about kick-points. A higher kick-point shaft is more likely to fly the ball a little bit lower than a low kick-point shaft. A lower kick-point shaft can, therefore, be advantageous to the player with more limited club-head speed. However, the strike of the ball on the clubface has far more effect on trajectory than the shaft ever will so, unless you are already a very consistent ball striker, don't stress too much over the exact specification of your shafts.

The exact shaft for you is dependent on many factors including your swing speed at impact with the ball, your overall tempo and how hard you accelerate the club form the top of your backswing. You should always seek the advice of your coach or club professional before you purchase a new club or consider a change of shaft.

4.11 Swing weight

There are two distinct weights to any golf club. One is the overall weight of the entire club when measured on a standard scale and the other is referred to as the 'swing weight'. As its name suggests, this is the weight you feel (or should feel ... see the chapter 'Swing; don't hit') during your swing and is a measure of the weight of the club-head in comparison to the overall weight of the club. Swing-weight is very much a personal preference but, in general terms, a heavier swing weight suits the more powerful player and a lighter swing-weight should be chosen for most lady players or more senior male golfers. Again, professional advice should be sought before investing your money.

4.12 Grip size

Incorrectly sized grips will have a detrimental effect on the way your club is held! The way you hold the club has more influence over your swing than any other factor and the correct sized grips are of paramount importance to your game. If your grips are too large for your hands then you are likely to hold the club too much in the palm of your hand. Too small and your fingers will dig into the butt of your hand as they wrap around the grip too much. I cannot stress enough how important a good grip of the club is in order for you to *become a better golfer*; incorrectly sized grips will only make achieving this more difficult.

4.13 A final word on equipment

Billions of Dollars, Pounds, Euros and Yen are spent on golf equipment around the world every year. How much of it is sensibly spent is anyone's guess, but I wager that very little of it is wisely spent? Most of the money is wasted on buying the very latest version of whatever club has just been updated ... very often less than a year since the previous model was launched. Yet more money is wasted on what looks like a great deal or is a heavily discounted item. Yes, it may appear to be a saving on the retail price, but little consideration is given to the suitability of the item for the player's level of play at that time. Very often these purchases make the player's golf even more difficult rather than easier. There is no miracle purchase, or wonder club, that will transform your game anywhere near as much as the marketing companies would have you believe. Indeed, every golf shot you strike is, inescapably, much more down to YOU and YOUR SWING than any club you will ever use!

CHAPTER 5

How to hold your clubs ... your grip for life!

5.1 A good grip is the inescapable requirement for a more natural swing

If you truly aspire to become a better golfer then you cannot afford to ignore this chapter. If you're starting from scratch, following the advice hereafter will help you to start your golfing 'career' with a proper hold on your clubs.

If you've been playing for a while, changing your grip can be tricky. Even a slight change in your grip will feel uncomfortable and unnatural at first (even though a good grip is a completely natural thing). Neither is a change in your grip likely to improve your golf shots immediately ... in fact your game is more likely to get worse in the short term. However, quite simply, better golf shots come from better swings and better swings come from better grips! A poor grip will lead to an unnatural and unnecessarily improvised swing and therefore make an already difficult game even harder.

Achieving a good grip will take practice, patience and perseverance. It may feel uncomfortable at first and, as with any change you make, you will need to be prepared for the possibility of even more inconsistent ball-striking while you get accustomed to your new grip. You will not, however, become the golfer you could have been unless your hands are placed nicely and correctly on the grip.

I say *'nicely'*, rather than *'perfectly'*, as there are slight variations in grip even amongst the best of players. However, their grips all look natural, comfortable and powerful … almost as if they were born with a golf club in their hands! Of course, they weren't! They had to acquire a *'nice'* hold of the club through learning and practice just as you will need to.

The teaching of the grip can often be over complicated and is most easily learned by copying the way we would naturally hold everyday objects. Sam Snead, a famous American golfer from the early nineteen-hundreds, went as far as to say *"if folks held their knives and forks like they hold their golf clubs, they would surely starve to death"*. This may seem a little extreme, but the way you hold everyday objects can tell you a lot about the way you should be holding your golf club. The items mentioned later in this chapter are examples of objects we hold throughout our lives that will remind us of how simple a good golf grip can be. In fact, I get the most success getting a pupil to understand this simply by handing them the grip end of a golf club and asking them to take it from me without thinking about anything to do with golf at all!

Most beginners, I see, have already been shown how to hold the club by someone else. Typically, by a well-meaning family member or friend who believes completely that they know how the club should be held. They might talk about the number of *'knuckles'* showing on your top hand or where the 'v' points on your bottom hand or that you should squeeze the grip just as you would hold a baby bird so it wouldn't fly away or be hurt. Honestly though, how many baby birds have you held recently?! This myth has been flying around for years (no pun intended!) but yes, you should hold the club gently and more in your fingers than in the palm of your hand. Your natural power is in the crook of your fingers and not in how securely you think you need to hold on to the club. If you hold the club in the palm of your hands you will need to

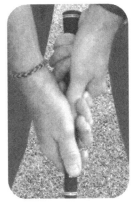

'*muscle*' the ball if you want to hit it a long way ... clearly not an option for lady golfers, older golfers or juniors (whom ironically often hit the ball much further anyway than their strength would suggest).

This point will be elaborated upon much more in the chapter '*Swing; don't hit*', but, succinctly put, if you can't hold the club 'nicely' you won't be able to swing the club 'nicely'. A good grip will enable you to feel the club's head

The 'palmy' grip ... the club has been 'grabbed'

through your fingers and therefore enable you to feel where the club-head is throughout your swing. You will then have a much better chance of swinging through the ball more cleanly and you will have a better chance of hitting more consistent golf shots.

So, go ahead and pick up these everyday objects ... including your golf clubs ... one hand at a time. Feel how '*Mother Nature*' intended your hands to fit around objects of a certain size and, above all, practice it over and over until it feels like second nature. It's not impossible to hit great golf shots with a poor grip but it is unlikely that you will ever reach your true potential unless you learn to hold the club in a natural, athletic, secure and potentially powerful way.

5.2 Everyday objects

In order to get both hands to fall naturally onto your  club, I want you to understand how your hands really work in everyday life. You will need to imagine  that you might also use your non-natural hand to accomplish these tasks as we need both hands working in harmony on your golf club. Use your natural  hand first and then replicate with the other hand to understand this principle. Note especially how  your hands fall naturally on top of the object and that there is a straight line through  your forearm and wrist. Our hands and wrists will not work efficiently if there is a 'kink' in the wrist or our palms are 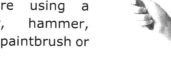 turned even slightly upwards.

So, whether you are using a toothbrush, screwdriver, hammer, bread-knife, watering can, paintbrush or any other everyday object, take a good look at the way your hands naturally work.

5.3 Your golf club

In the same natural way that we pick up other everyday objects pick up your golf club in the same

manner. Or, better still, ask someone to hand you your golf club (grip first) and just take it from them without thinking ... first in one hand and then the other. You will almost certainly take the club from them with a perfectly natural hold. Feel perhaps that you are simply shaking hands with the club.

Take the club first in one hand ...

Once you have understood the simplicity of this and have understood how natural the hold on your golf club should be, we can now begin to add a little bit more precision to the art of holding the club. I use the word art here as there is a real subtlety to the way we should hold our golf club and feel its weight throughout the swing.

... and then the other

You will already have learnt that we hold most things in the crook of our fingers or the base of our fingers. This is where the strength in our hands lies and where the sensation of *'feel'* comes from. We have little or no sensation of feel from the palms of our hands, but this is where the vast majority of golfers seem to want to place the club. This seems to offer a misplaced feeling of muscle power and the added security that they won't let go of the club. They may also worry that the feeling of the club twisting within their hands at impact is due to their grip being too loose. However, this twisting is caused by an off-centre strike when the sudden force of striking the toe or heel of the club will wrench the club from even the most perfect of grips. Do not be tempted therefore to squeeze the club harder in order to avoid this inevitable consequence of an off-centre strike on the clubface.

To reiterate the point, we weren't really '*designed*' to hold anything in the palm of our hands ... there is no dexterity or feel there. Neither will our wrists or forearms work effectively throughout our golf swing without a natural hold of the golf club ... they will end up hindering one another during the swing. Nor were our thumbs ever designed to be separated from the rest of the hand when we hold things. Therefore, ensure that you keep your thumbs adjacent to the forefinger of each hand as you take your grip.

Note that, with virtually everything we hold, our hands are positioned with the palms angled slightly downwards. In many players, I see the palms facing upwards as if they have '*grabbed*' the club rather than deftly placing their hands naturally upon it. The natural position evolves from the way our hands and forearms simply hang naturally when we are standing and relaxed. Notice how your thumbs fall inwards towards your legs and your palms face slightly backwards. The exact position varies from person to person but everyone is similar enough for this to be the basis for your natural grip (refer to the everyday objects again and again until you fully appreciate these details).

5.4 Taking your grip when you play

Now, take your golf club and place it in the correct playing position using the hand which will be the lower hand on your club. Leave plenty of room for your top hand to be placed in position. Bring your top hand from your side, being very careful not to rotate your forearm or 'kink' your wrist in any way, and place it gently on the grip, wrapping your fingers softly around it. Return

Set the club in position and then add each hand gently in turn

your bottom hand to your side and bring it carefully back to the club ... again without any forearm rotation or wrist-kink. Don't worry about overlapping or interlocking any fingers at this stage; simply cover the top hand thumb with your bottom hand ... your top thumb should fit nicely into the palm of your bottom hand. Repeat this process over and over until comfortable and natural, gradually increasing the speed at which you can achieve this. Try closing your eyes as you do it and feel how your hands are placed. Keep doing it until a good grip becomes your predominant habit.

Practising your grip is best done away from the golf course or driving range; therefore, do it at home. Leave a club handy in the house so you can practice regularly. Just five or ten minutes a day for a few weeks will transform your grip from the claw-like disaster it may once have been, into an artful thing of beauty and precision. A honed and natural grip will allow and encourage your whole body to work in harmony with all its moving parts ... consequently helping to increase club-head speed through impact and fine-tune your ball-striking skill.

You will now have enough knowledge to refine the way you hold your golf clubs and be much better placed to understand some of the usual golf terminology regarding the grip. Here are some more precise definitions of what is meant by the usual clichéd and often misunderstood phrases we hear all the time.

5.5 The V's, knuckles, placement and precision

You will no doubt have heard or read about the hand positions on the golf club expressed in terms of either, how many knuckles you can see on the backs of your hands, or where your V's should be pointing in relation to your shoulder. What is generally misunderstood, however, is how these positions are achieved or what position the knuckles and V's should be viewed from.

Hopefully, by now, you will have grasped the concept (no pun intended!) of how the grip of your golf club should nestle naturally into the crook of your fingers … as if holding any other everyday object. The exact positioning of your hands and particularly how far one way or the other they might be rotated to your left or right has a huge influence over whether you pull, push, hook or slice your ball. In fact, it's probably the number one factor involved (hence the detail and length of this chapter).

The photos in the following sections show the ideal grip and also some of the most common less-than-ideal ways to hold your golf club.

5.5.1 The V's

As the pictures show, the V is the shape that is formed between your forefinger and thumb of each hand. The V is formed between the top part of your thumb (i.e. the nail-end) and the bottom part (or base) of your forefinger. The lower half of your thumb should fit snugly against your hand below the base of your forefinger forming a line or crevice that leads into the V. This detail is very important because, if your thumb gets separated from the rest of your hand, you will lose control and power. If your thumb is wayward on your top hand you will not be able to place your bottom hand correctly. Worse still, your thumb may find its way around the back of the grip which is a really ineffective way of holding anything. If in doubt, keep returning to those everyday objects to experience how your hands and thumbs work naturally.

The first thing to ensure is that the V's on both of your hands line up with each other. This guarantees

that your hands will, at least, be working for each other and not fighting against one another as you swing the club. If your V's don't line up, you cannot generate as much club-head speed as you could. The result will be much compensation within your swing.

The ideal grip. Note visible watch-face and 3 'knuckles'

Once your V's are in line with each other we can focus on how your hands are orientated on the grip: that is, where should the line through your V's point in relation to you. The photos show examples of good and poor grips. The ideal grip would have the line drawn through your V's pointing up the inside of your lower arm towards that shoulder. This is deemed a neutral grip where your hands, wrists and forearms will work effectively throughout your swing and optimise your club-head speed and clubface angle through impact.

Correct grip (with glove) showing V's aligning with the inside of your lower arm

If your hands are rotated too much one way or the other around the handle then problems will occur. If

rotated excessively around the grip towards the target you will be prone to slicing, hitting the ball higher than expected, and generally losing distance. Hence this type of grip is commonly known as a *'weak'* grip. If rotated excessively around the other way you will be prone to hooking and pulling and your shots will lack sufficient

Weak grip - hands rotated too far around towards the target

elevation for the ball to land softly and stop

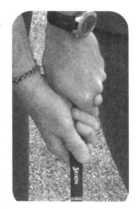

where you want it to. This incorrect grip is known, conversely, as a *'strong'* grip. This is also not ideal, but as its name suggests it is much more preferable to the *'weak'* grip described above and is a more common bad habit amongst already pretty good players.

Strong grip: hands rotated too far away from the target ... too many knuckles!

5.5.2 The Knuckles

This final point on the grip describes another way to check that your hands are in the right position. This concept is usually a check-point for the top hand and relates to how many knuckles should be seen when your grip is viewed by someone else (preferably someone who knows what they are looking for) or by yourself when facing a mirror.

As the photo of the ideal grip shows, being able to see three of the knuckles on the back of your top hand when viewed from the front is my recommendation for the top hand grip. Most written coaching suggests two to three knuckles showing on the top hand, but I have observed too many *weak* top hand positions and a trait of better players and especially longer hitters is to have a *stronger* grip. Once again, go back to those everyday objects we discussed earlier in this chapter and experiment by rotating your hand into the wrong positions and see how you lack mobility, power and control of the implement you are holding.

One last thought. If golf was a one-handed game … how would you hold the club? Try swinging your club one-handed; first with your natural bottom hand and then with your usual top hand. I guarantee you will hold (the club) each time with an almost perfect and natural grip. Now blend both of your hands together on the club in the same natural way. Your grip is as simple as this, but I must emphasise once again that if you want to develop the *better player* that lives within you … you must develop a good grip.

In Summary, a better grip WILL improve your golf. Maybe, or maybe not, straight away, but you cannot (and I don't use that word very often) reach your true potential without a natural hold on your golf club. A weak, sloppy or untidy grip will lead to weak, sloppy and untidy golf. A good grip offers more leverage in the swing, higher club-head speed, improved feel of the club and more control over the clubface angle ... in short, better golf!

CHAPTER 6

Swing, don't hit!

6.1 Let the club do the work

'Let the ball get in the way of your swing'. *'Let the club do the work'*. You've probably heard these old adages many times and they have almost become clichés in themselves, but what do they really mean? The club clearly isn't going to hit the ball for you and you can't ignore the ball completely, but how have these old expressions (probably the oldest) lasted so long? They are also as appropriate today as they were at the *'dawn of golfing time'*.

Despite the incredible advances in technology (which the marketing people would have you believe is the answer to all your prayers), it is always YOU that will have the primary influence over where your golf ball ends up! However, it's not how diligently or perfectly mechanically you attempt to swing the club but that your swing is actually just that ... A SWING and not a wild swipe or hit at the ball.

The most common bad habit I witness in the golf swing is hitting AT the ball as opposed to swinging THROUGH it (i.e. letting the ball get in the way). The desire to hit the ball a long way invites us to (almost involuntarily) take a wild *'swipe'* at the ball. In fact, the reasoning that the harder you hit the ball the further it will go is a perfectly logical one in your early days of playing golf. It seems logical that there must be a huge effort involved in order to hit the ball a long way or that it must be sheer muscle power that allows the top players to hit the ball so far. However, if this was the case then all great golfers would be built like wrestlers and talented twelve-year-olds wouldn't be able to hit the ball well over 200 yards already.

So, if it's not brute strength that propels the ball into *'the middle of next week'* then what is it? How, at the same time, can we keep the ball relatively straight without falsely manipulating the club face? The answer is precision timing. Like every ball sport you can think of, the timing of your swing through the ball is crucial to the speed and direction the ball leaves your hand, foot, bat, or racket. Good timing tends to cover up a multitude of other *'sins'* in any technique … all good players of any sport have great rhythm and good timing.

In golfing terms, what do we mean by good timing? The ball is stationary before we swing, so it should be easier, right? Wrong! The slower a ball is travelling the more time we have to think about the process of striking a ball and the more unnatural and less instinctive it becomes. Think of the *'dolly-drop'* return in tennis, for example, that bounces gently and invitingly in front of you, only for you to over-think what you're going to do and you end up *'dunching'* the shot into the net. Or the footballer who is six yards away from an almost unprotected goal and somehow manages to miss the target completely. The reason for these disastrous misses is down to the extra time we have to think about what we're about to do. It becomes less instinctive and more thoughtful and mechanical. In golf, we have more time to think than almost any other sport you can name. In moving-ball sports we react in a more natural and decisive way. In golf, it is easy to over-analyse and be tentative during the swing for fear of making a poor shot.

In this chapter, I want to help you to understand your natural swing and to steer you away from complex swing thoughts and swing mechanics. Until you are able to swing the club fluently, rhythmically and consistently, at the same tempo, any thoughts of complicated swing mechanics will be impossible to implement. However, before we explore the swing in more detail, I would like to reiterate the importance of the grip and also emphasise the significance of how you stand to the ball.

6.2 The Stance

Also referred to as your 'set-up' or 'address', how you stand BEFORE you swing will have a profound effect on HOW you swing. A lot is written about the stance and the precision of how you should set up to the ball, but, in my experience, this can be over-complicated to the point where players (literally) tie themselves in knots in the attempt to achieve the ideal body alignment, club-face aim and posture. The better the player, the more precise the set-up should be. However, if you're new to the game or relatively inexperienced, a comfortable, relaxed and un-contorted stance is all you need.

The following images show the ideal set-up position and also some less desirable ones ... ones which tend to be the most common.

Stance too far away and posture far too crouched with hands consequently too low

Set-up position too upright with hands forced unnaturally high

Too close

The ideal posture at set-up ... strong but relaxed

Ideal set-up from the front view

Set up for the driver is different

Provided you are standing sideways to your target, with the ball appropriately positioned for the club you have selected (see ball positions in 'technical stuff'), you are already half-way there. With your feet roughly shoulder width apart, your knees slightly flexed (kind of 'bouncy', but not 'sat' down) and your back tilted slightly forward, you should easily be able to place the club-head behind the ball. Also, ensure that your arms are straight and the bottom of the club is flat on the ground and you will be in a pretty good position already. You will now be in a relaxed, but ready, state and able to swing the club freely.

The more proficient a player you become, the more important your stance becomes, and the more specific the requirements. The better golfer will usually already have a very strong set-up position and a well-practised stance. This better player will have a straight back and straight arms; a position of power from which you can maximise your efforts efficiently. Your weight should be on the balls of your feet in a 'ready to go' kind of balance. Your weight should never be on your heels ... this is a recipe for losing your balance and therefore losing control.

6.3 Your new grip ... feel the club

At this point, I want to reiterate the importance of the grip. Without a 'nice' hold on your club, as described previously, you won't be able to feel the head of the club throughout the swing, and you won't be able to maximise the speed your club-head is travelling at as it makes contact with the ball.

I hope by now you will have practised and amended your grip sufficiently to understand its significance in the evolution of your golf swing. Your grip is your connection with your club and your club's connection with you. If there is one secret to the golf swing it is being able to feel, picture and imagine where the head of your golf club is throughout the motion. This is no different to any sport that involves a club, racket, stick, or bat ... it's just that your golf 'bat' is significantly smaller than all the other ones so it's even more critical that you 'know' (can feel) where it is.

One of the best ways to feel the true weight and position of your golf club, in relation to you, is to swing the golf club with one hand at a time. It is more natural to swing one-handed and you will get a true sense of how your body reacts when making this swing. The following section is, therefore, the most important thing to understand and implement into your technique.

6.4 Swish to the finish

I once heard the golf swing described as 'two turns and a swish' and this statement couldn't describe the core of teaching any better. I would never describe golf as easy (in fact far from it), but the golf swing itself is a relatively straightforward and simple series of human motions.

Your natural swing comprises just a few core movements which all great players have within their swings. As suggested earlier, many of these great players have far from textbook techniques but they all have the same common denominators within their swings.

So, what are these common themes and how can you ensure they are incorporated in your own swing? The simple drill described and pictured below will give you a very quick feel for the natural 'ebb and flow' we should feel throughout. By holding the club at the head end of the shaft and one-handed (using your usual bottom hand as it lies on the grip) I want you to forget for a minute any of your current beliefs about the golf swing. By holding the club in this way, with your 'natural' hand, a more natural and free-flowing swing will result (see note below regarding left-handed versus right-handed, especially if your bottom hand on the grip is not the one you would naturally throw a ball with, play tennis with etc.).

6.5 The Drill

Hold the golf club upside down with your hand on the shaft just beneath the club-head and sideways to your imaginary target in the normal golfing way. Simply think of swinging the grip end of the club backwards and forwards with the intention of making a loud 'wooshing' noise as it 'swishes' towards your target ... quite a satisfying sound, isn't it? The louder you try to make this sound, and the more freely you swing, the more your natural swing will emerge. The key points I want you to recognise in this drill are as follows.

Hold any club just beneath the club-head to perform this drill. Forget about playing golf and swing 'the stick' backwards and forwards with the intention of making a loud 'swish' or 'woosh' with the grip. The phrase 'swish to the finish' should always be at the forefront of your mind when you play.

'Throw' everything you've got towards the target and you will appreciate the natural momentum in a natural swing of a 'stick'. Swing right through to a full finish ... feel how everything flows and how naturally you will achieve our intended 'trophy' finish position.

Try the same drill with the club the normal way up. You will also appreciate the true weight of the golf club in this way.

Most importantly, feel how your weight shifting forwards leads the club

6.5.1 Body turn

You could probably 'swish' the club using just your arm, but in order to maximise the power you can achieve (i.e. maximise the noise you hear) your body will want to naturally 'wind up' or coil as you take the club away. Then as you swish the grip towards your target your body will naturally unwind adding more speed. In effect, two turns and a swish as described above.

6.5.2 Elbow bend

You could swing the club in this way with your arm straight, but it wouldn't be the most effective way to generate speed. When you play other one-handed sports such as tennis, badminton, squash, table tennis and when throwing a ball, the arm will bend to create more leverage in the action. Therefore, allow your arm to relax naturally at the elbow as you swing away into your backswing.

6.5.3 Wrist cock

This is a widely misunderstood action within your golf swing. You shouldn't intentionally bend your wrists in the backswing, neither should you deliberately inhibit your wrists from hinging as you swing. The wrist cock will happen naturally provided that you have a good grip and you allow your elbow to bend as described above. Again, think of other sports you may have played or simple actions such as using a paintbrush or hammer and you will understand wrist-cock.

6.5.4 Weight shift

Feel how your weight wants to shift naturally from foot to foot as you swing. You will instinctively rock onto your back foot (the furthest foot from the target) as you take the club away and then back onto your front foot as you 'swish' the club through. If you don't hold back and let your weight flow through towards your imaginary target, you will end up in the classic golf finish that every better player has always displayed.

6.5.5 The finish

It is no coincidence that every good and great player ends up in pretty much the same position after every full shot swing. I have heard it argued that the ball has already been hit by then, so why is it so important? The finish position, however, is the direct result of every minuscule action that preceded it and is a product of a full and powerful motion. The pictures below show the classic golf position and although you may feel you already achieve this position, take a closer look and ask yourself these questions.

1. Are you completely balanced? Or is there a wobble?
2. Is your back foot right up onto the point of its toe with the sole of the foot facing backwards?
3. Is ALL your weight on your front foot?
4. Are your hips square to the target? (I.e. at right angles to a line drawn back from the target through you).
5. Are your hands high above your lead shoulder? (left shoulder if you're right-handed and right shoulder if you're left-handed)

A well-balanced finish with all your weight on your front foot and hips square to the target

71

These positions all add up to a well-balanced and free-flowing finish which will be the result of a solid and consistently well-timed swing ... and consistency is what you're searching for. Is it not?

I cannot stress how important this drill is in helping you to understand your natural swing and to help you feel how simple the golf swing really is. By that, I mean the swing is relatively simple ... the game, unfortunately, is not.

You should keep practising this drill until all the movements within it feel comfortable and

Your back foot should be right up on the point of the toes

repeatable. If performed sufficiently and without any thoughts of your old swing, you will soon feel confident in this new motion.

Now try swinging the club the right way up but still with one hand. You will now appreciate how heavy your club actually is ... not so easily appreciated with both hands on the grip. The weight you feel is almost entirely on the head end

You should be completely facing the target at the end of your swing

of the club and, as this is obviously the part of the golf club that strikes the ball, you need to be able to feel where it is throughout your swing. Swinging with one hand in this way allows you to understand how the forces in the swing can work in your favour. Perhaps try hitting some shots with just one hand on the grip and you will appreciate even more how to use the club's weight most efficiently. Tee the ball up slightly for this task and don't use anything longer than a seven-iron. Your first few shots will probably go astray as you struggle with the extra weight, but you will soon adapt and will be pleasantly surprised at how far you can hit the ball with just one hand.

The trick now is to introduce your top hand into the swing without interrupting the flow of your new natural swing. This is where your new grip will be tested to the max. In order for your bottom hand to swing the club naturally, your top hand must comply and allow this to happen. The positioning, therefore, of each hand, is critical to how you can perform the swing.

Continue the drill, now with the club the right way around, and with both hands on the grip. Listen for the swish the club makes as it seems to pull you into a full and flowing finish. Hold this finish for a count of three. Remember how it feels to be balanced and in control of your club and yet you were able to make an impressive 'woosh' with the club-head as it swished through to that finish. The louder this noise, the more club-head speed you are generating, and it is speed in the club which is the primary force in determining distance. However, you must be balanced throughout your swing as striking the ball from the 'sweet spot' on the club is almost equally influential in how far your ball goes. If you are not balanced at the end (of your swing), it is unlikely you were in control through impact with the ball and your power and ball-striking will be compromised.

As you play, and practise, keep reminding yourself of this drill and keep going back to it … it really is the best way of ensuring you SWING and don't HIT.

6.5.6 Left hand or right handed for this drill

A surprising number of people play golf right-handed or left-handed but with their natural hand at the top of the grip (your natural hand being the one you would predominantly use to accomplish one-handed tasks, such as catching/throwing a ball, playing squash, badminton, tennis or cleaning your teeth!). If this describes you then you can still perform this drill to give you the best feel for your natural swing … albeit the other way around! You are essentially playing golf 'back-hand' in the same way as you would play a back-hand in racket sports.

6.6 Rhythm is the answer

In whatever fashion you swing the club, and however 'perfectly' you might do it, if you don't swing the club at precisely the same speed every time your results will be inconsistent. It might seem strange, but hitting a ball that is not moving is infinitely more difficult than hitting a ball that has been propelled towards you. The reason is simple. When a ball is still we have too much time to think, and the more time we have to think, the more unnatural and counter-intuitive the motion tends to be. Think of a penalty kick in football or hockey, a simple pot in snooker, the second serve in tennis or even throwing a dart ... or indeed any action that is one hundred percent down to YOU. Not being at the mercy of anyone else creates a completely self-induced pressure to perform and succeed. There is no-one else to blame if you miss. There are no extenuating circumstances that should hinder your performance. In other words, there is a unique pressure and, in golf, every shot you play has this pressure attached to it ... assuming you care where the ball goes that is!

Although a good swing and sound technique are important, even a perfect swing performed by a robot will not hit the ball accurately, or as far as it could, if the timing of the robot's swing varies even slightly. If there is any single common denominator amongst top performers in any sport it is exquisite timing. The ability to perform the same motion at the same speed and tempo virtually every time (especially under pressure) leads them to more consistent performance.

6.7 More concepts to help you

'Swish to the finish' is one concept, but how else can we think about our golf swing in order to keep it rhythmical, flowing, co-ordinated and balanced?

Your swing should 'build' from the start to the finish. It should 'build' in intensity and speed and be able to deliver maximum speed as your golf club makes contact with the ball. If this maximum speed is in the right place, and at the right time, then your swing will take you automatically to the classic trophy finish as described earlier in this chapter.

You could also think of your swing in musical terms. If RHYTHM is one of the key points, think of a tune, a line in a song, or any phrase which has enough syllables (and therefore beats) to fit with the natural tempo of your swing. Some people have quicker tempos in life than others. Some walk with quick steps and speak quickly whilst others are more languid and don't rush anything they do. Your tempo should, therefore, reflect your personality ... to some extent at least. So, find a tune, rhyme or lyric that fits your natural tempo and you will always have something to fall back on.

Continuing the musical theme, think of the musical term crescendo, meaning 'a progressive increase in volume and intensity'. If you think of your swing in this way, gradually building the intensity (or effort) until it reaches a climax as you 'swish' through the ball to the finish, you will achieve a progressively accelerating motion. Once again, the operative word here is THROUGH ... we must swing THROUGH the ball and not AT it.

Another analogy might be to think of a racing car or motorbike on a long straight road approaching from a distance: the sound building gradually and then increasing dramatically as it passes you by ... only to diminish gradually as it passes out of sight. You might even say 'v...r...ooooom' to yourself as you swing. Also, think of the tennis player who grunts as he or she powers through the ball ... the sound (or grunt) is the result of the effort and is after impact with the ball and not before. You probably won't want to be audibly 'grunting' or 'vrooming' around the golf course (though you might just start a new craze!), but you can certainly be thinking about these concepts as you swing: these are far better thoughts and feelings than anything mechanical or technical. Above everything else, your swing must flow.

6.8 Practise swing versus ball striking swing

Show me a top player who doesn't make some kind of practise swing and I'll stop doing what I'm doing. If you're watching on TV, you won't always see the practise swing as it may happen off camera or the footage cuts straight to a player already in position to execute the shot, but there will some kind of rehearsal swing for sure. Sometimes, this swing is nothing more than an exaggerated *waggle* (see glossary) of the club-head, but, at the very least, this gives you a feel for the club you are about to use (one which you may not have used for some time or not yet during your round that day).

Despite this obvious trait of better players, I don't know how many times I've heard people say that they've stopped using a practise swing because they feel their practise swing is okay but that the swing they use to hit the ball is totally different. The truth is, our ball striking swing will always be slightly different to our practise swing, but the closer it is in rhythm, flow and tempo to the swing we have just rehearsed the better.

So, let's think of that practise swing more in terms of a rehearsal swing or dry run. It won't be an exact replica of the swing you use to hit the ball, but that shouldn't stop you rehearsing the swing you would like to use to play the shot. Also, let's face it, the game is difficult enough and stop-start enough, already, without us being expected to just walk up to the ball and make a perfect swing ... the best players don't do it so neither should you.

Your practise/rehearsal swing can achieve many things to help with the shot at hand if you're using it correctly. It's your opportunity to get the 'thinking' bit out of the way; to rehearse the actions you've been learning or practising on the driving range. It's your opportunity to get the feel for the club you are about to use. It's your opportunity to listen for the swish of the club as you swing to your 'trophy finish'. It's your opportunity to feel how your body moves throughout the swing and how, and when, you should deliver the power through the ball. In short, you'd be mad not to do it.

So, if you are happy with your practice swing, what makes you do something that is sometimes completely different when you hit the ball? The answer is, the ball itself. The ball interrupts your swing. The ball becomes the absolute focus of your eyes and your attention. The ball becomes the target and the actual target gets forgotten ... the ball makes us hit AT it instead of THROUGH it. Hitting AT, or into, the ball is the reason you don't get to the same position at the end of your swing as you did when you practised it ... hence the reason you give up on your practise swings as you feel they are a waste of time. The following section will offer you some simple solutions to this common dilemma.

6.9 How to avoid hitting AT the ball

As described above, hitting AT the ball is probably the most common cause of mishit, misdirected and distance-limited golf shots. Hitting hard at the ball requires maximum acceleration from the top of your backswing with your effort being directed into the ball rather than through the ball. By definition, you cannot have maximum effort/power in two places at once and your club-head speed through contact with the ball will not be as high as it could be. We don't deliberately or consciously try to hit hard AT the ball, it just happens through a combination of panic, anxiousness, over-aggression or a simple lack of belief, or trust, in your swing. It's hard for anyone to trust in their swing completely as, for all players of all abilities, it goes wrong a lot. But trust IN it we must, as it's all we have at the time of executing the shot. Your swing will have flaws, faults and quirky bits within it (show me someone's that doesn't), but your swing is more than capable of hitting great shots consistently if you let it.

Let's consider, for a minute, how blind players play golf? ... and yes, blind players can and do play exceptional golf. The best of them shoot scores in the low 70's and have very low handicaps, but how is this possible? The easiest thing about golf should be that the ball doesn't move ... so it is in some ways 'at your mercy' and therefore makes it more possible than some sports for a blind person to play golf well. However, one of the hardest things about golf is also that, the ball doesn't move. A blind player is probably more adept at feeling his or her swing and the ball has much less influence on the emphasis of the swing as it cannot become the target for the strike. For the sighted player, however, it becomes all too easy to see the ball as the object of our desire (or loathing!) and therefore for the emphasis (or effort) in our swing to be directed AT the ball ... as opposed to focusing the effort on the entire swing and the 'trophy' finish.

Here are some other thoughts that may help you achieve a swing rather than a hit.

6.10 Imagine your 'trophy finish' throughout your swing

We are all guilty of thinking about far too many things during our golf swings. Sometimes there may be four or five things going on in our heads at the same time, but, as the average golf swing lasts only for approximately 1.6 seconds, not even Albert Einstein would be capable of managing more than a thought or two in that space of time ... although we can FEEL the thoughts if we allow ourselves to. If 'a picture paints a thousand words' (Fred R Barnard, 1921) then how many thoughts can a feeling convey? The feeling you get from your practise swing is more than enough ... provided you perform it with a purpose. There are dozens of thoughts wrapped up in one golf swing and your practise swing is your opportunity to think and, more importantly, feel some of those thoughts. You MUST, however, use the FEELING and not the thoughts as you commit your swing to the ball. So, as you feel your swing in your rehearsal/practise swing, you must be able to convey this feeling into the swing you use to strike the ball with ... and the thought of where you need to be at the end of your swing is as powerful as any.

As you make a practise swing (either before you hit the ball on the course or when practising on the range), be sure to envisage, feel and imagine the position you should be in at the end of your swing. I hear so often that the finish is way after the ball has been struck, so why does it matter? Where you finish at the end of your swing is the direct result of everything that came before it ... a kind of 'chicken and egg' scenario ... you can't have one without the other.

6.11 Counting, humming, singing and swinging

To be consistent (the magic word in golf) you must do consistent things and you must swing with a consistent rhythm. Rhythm, as mentioned before, is a musical, almost mystical thing, but everyone has it. Most people can count to the beat of a song or dance to the rhythm of a piece of music and this ability can be useful in swinging your golf club at a consistent speed and tempo (time and time again).

Many great players have thought, sung or hummed some strange things as they swing, but why would they do this? Even great players lose their rhythm from time to time and this is often the main reason for a dip in form. Sometimes this can be caused by just one bad shot, one bad hole or one bad day, leading to a loss of confidence in their swing. It is rarely the mechanics of the swing that suddenly change but this loss of confidence slowly leads to a lack of belief in the swing and results in the common fault of hitting AT the ball in desperation ... as opposed to swinging smoothly THROUGH it. Therefore, the confident smooth rhythm of the successful player is replaced by a hesitant or rushed attack at the ball ... a kind of panic that sets in resulting from the fear of missing the shot ... 'ballitis' as I once heard it very appropriately described!

So, how do these players (or we) get the rhythm back? You, almost certainly, cannot play a round of golf without losing your rhythm at least once or twice; getting it back in time for the next shot is crucial to recovering or keeping your round going. We, therefore, need a mechanism for rapid recovery from an errant shot (or a mishit chip or missed putt ... both equally as susceptible to a loss in rhythm as is our full swing). We need a way of recognising that we have mistimed a swing and a way of ensuring that it doesn't happen again on the next shot. Finding a mantra that fits the rhythm of your good swings is the key.

This mantra could take many forms. It could be as simple as counting to a rhythm that fits your swing. It could be a line or two, or bar or two from a favourite song. It could be a 'tick-tock' or click-click ... but something with more than two 'beats' is preferable, such as ... 'back-and-through' or 'swing-back-swing-through'. It could be anything that's personal to you but you must recognise it when you're swinging well and be able to remember it when things are going wrong. This personal mantra can also be really effective when you are nervous or under extra pressure on the course ... keep repeating it to yourself, both during your practise swings and also when you are swinging to hit the ball.

Your personal mantra could also be a visual one or, perhaps, an audible one. Visualising the smooth swinging motion of a pendulum or a swing-boat from a fairground ride can reinforce the mental image you have of a good swing. Listening for the swish or woosh of the club in your practise swing, or the sound of the grass being clipped as you practise for a chip or pitch, can be helpful when endeavouring to repeat your rhythm accurately when you play the shot itself. It's worth spending some time experimenting with these notions when you practise

6.12 In summary of 'swing don't hit'

If you start with a good grip, a natural stance and a smooth rhythmical motion ending in a full and balanced finish every time ... your golf will improve. If you keep focused on these principals you will very quickly look like a better golfer ... and of course, better golfers look like better golfers, don't they?!

CHAPTER 7

The short-game swing

7.1 What is the short-game?

The short-game encompasses the variety of shots you need to play when approaching the green that do not require full power from even the shortest iron in your set. In other words, when your normal swing will hit the ball too far with your shortest club, you need a different technique.

Many new players simply try to hit the ball more softly using the only swing they know at this stage of their development. The common result is either a complete mishit or a shot that invariably goes much too far because the swing was much too long.

Start your quest for a better short game with this thought in mind ... your short game swing is very different from your full swing or power game swing (i.e. the swing you use to hit each of your clubs as far as they will go) and, therefore, requires a different technique and practise regime.

Your short-game swing, as the phrase suggests, requires a shorter swing. A swing that will propel the ball to varying distances but never up to the full potential of the club you are using ... that's your power-game swing. This shorter swing, however, must still accelerate smoothly through contact with the ball and we must endeavour not to hit AT the ball as described earlier for your full swing ... 'swing, don't hit' still being the operative feeling here. Though a shorter overall swing, the follow through should always be longer than the backswing. The longer follow through ensures that the club is accelerating smoothly through impact … it also ensures that the weight of the club remains under control through the strike.

Throughout this chapter, I will explain various ways of thinking about your short-game swing, but, essentially, it boils down to three overriding factors.

1. You must strike the ball cleanly from somewhere near the middle of the clubface.
2. Your club face must be pointing in the right direction as you strike the ball.
3. Your club must be travelling at the appropriate speed for the length of shot required.

Sounds simple enough, doesn't it? However, in practice, this is the part of the game with which most players struggle the most. It seems that the shorter the shot the more inconsistent the result and the more your mind will play tricks on you.

7.2 Chip or pitch?

One of the areas of constant confusion seems to surround the terminology used to describe the different types of shot you play on the golf course. One of the most commonly misunderstood, is the difference between a chip shot and a pitch shot. It is even described in different ways by different coaching professionals and even means different things in different countries. So, let's forget the different terms of description and settle on just one. I like to describe all short game shots as 'pitches' of some kind, rather than worrying about the semantics of language, as it keeps things simple ... golf is difficult enough without these peripheral confusions.

The word pitch has many meanings, but, in a ball sport, it means to deliver a ball to a target; to toss, throw, fling, launch or lob something in a relatively accurate and controlled way. Even with your hand and arm alone, you can throw (pitch) a ball different distances and at different heights and trajectories ... you could even roll a ball along the ground. In golf, the requirements for the shorter shots, as you approach the green, will be varied. You may be very close to the green or still some distance away. There may be a hazard to negotiate, or you may have a clear path to the flag. You may have plenty of putting green surface available to land your ball on, or there may not be much room between the closest edge of the green and the flag.

You will, therefore, need to play low shots, high shots, running shots and quickly stopping shots ... all with longer or shorter variations. But let's call them all pitches as it makes life a lot easier.

7.3 How to choose the appropriate shot

There is one overriding mantra for short-game shots which should help you decide the right shot to play. Always picture the ball landing on the green, bouncing and then rolling up to the hole, keeping the ball as low as possible to the ground whenever you can ... but why?

A ball that lands on the green is landing on a relatively flat and smooth surface of known texture and speed (assuming you've practised a little before you play) and will usually provide the truest initial bounce. Keeping the ball close to the ground increases the chances of a straight (true) bounce and is less at the mercy of excessive, or underestimated, backspin. Keeping the ball low means you can use a club with a lower loft ... a lower lofted club being easier to strike purely, more consistently. Using a more lofted club and expecting the ball to stop quickly adds a much higher degree of difficulty to the shot. There are, of course, occasions when a higher-flying, softer-landing shot is required, but should only be selected on 'needs must' basis.

7.4 Your Short Game Swing

I will start by explaining the things that often go wrong with our attempted short-game shots ... the bad habits if you like. The most common problem of all is the inconsistency in striking the ball cleanly. Most shots, for new players and even much experienced and otherwise accomplished players, seem to be either 'topped', 'thinned', 'fatted', 'toed', 'shanked' or some other, yet unnamed, misdemeanour. These are all negative terms, but we need to be clear about what we mean by them as many players get confused about why their ball ends up short of the green, skews off at acute angles, or hurtles through the green at 100 miles per hour! The main cause of these missed shots is down to where, on the clubface, the ball was struck. Here is a brief description of what we mean by fat, thin, topped, fatted etc. It is really important to understand these contacts as you will not otherwise be able to build up a good 'feel' for the power required if you are not striking the ball cleanly. For example; you probably haven't hit the ball too hard if your ball shoots off the back of the green, or too soft if your ball ends up in a bunker short of the green … it's more than likely that you mishit the shot.

1. Topped, thinned, skulled or knifed: These terms describe a contact with the ball that is higher than the desired point of impact. The result is a shot that either bobbles along the ground or flies much too low and lands without any backspin and shoots forward … usually much further than intended … but you almost certainly didn't hit the ball too hard.

2. Fat, fatted, chunked, duffed etc: All describe a contact where the club strikes the ground before the ball. The ball may fly low because your club has bounced off the ground and struck the ball too high up, or digs into the ground before the ball and saps all the energy and intended speed from the club-head before it reaches the ball. The ball invariably ends up way short of the target … but you probably haven't hit it too softly.

3. Toed: This is when the ball comes off the outer edge of the clubface (the toe) and shoots off at a tangent (to the right if you're right-handed). This is normally caused by the *toe* of the club closing in towards the ball too early.

4. Shanked: The causes of the 'shank' shot have been debated for decades but, whatever the cause, it is a mishit that shoots wildly to the right (if you're right-handed) but comes off the hosel of the club-head (the rounded corner at the heel end of your club) as opposed to the *toe* as described above. It's often been suggested that a shank is the nearest thing to a perfect shot (as the sweet spot is closer to the heel, or shank, of the club than the actual geometric centre of the clubface) but it certainly doesn't look like a perfect shot!! More detail on the 'shank' in chapter 13.4)

So, if all these contacts or non-contacts are undesirable, what terms describe the proper contact with the ball, as many players simply do not seem to understand how a good strike should feel. A good strike comes off the 'sweet spot' on the clubface. All sporting implements (rackets, bats, sticks or clubs) have a sweet spot and it's named in this way because it provides the addictive feeling of wanting to achieve it again and again. It is the memory of this feeling, as we swing, that gives us the best chance of finding that sweet spot more consistently.

If you are not yet sure how it feels, it's almost as if you don't feel the ball at all as it comes off the clubface. It's the result of the ball being struck from the exact 'centre of gravity' of the lump of metal (the club-head) that you are using to hit the ball. It is also the result of a perfectly timed swing ... whether using a full power swing or your new short-game swing.

7.5 Short-game swing technique

Now that you have a better understanding of good

strikes and miss-hits, we will discuss the flaws in technique that cause the poorly struck and misdirected shots.

Many mishits are caused by badly timed swings. That is, the club either accelerates too quickly or wildly into the ball, or the club

Leaning back attempting to 'lift' the ball in the air is a common mistake.

is decelerating as it makes contact with the ball. This either causes the club

to dig into the ground before the ball, or strikes the ball halfway up causing it to shoot along the ground.

Many other mishits are caused by attempting to 'lift' or 'scoop' the ball into the air by using a shovelling action with the wrists, or by leaning backwards through impact in a desperate attempt to get under the ball. We should never be attempting

Attempting to 'scoop' the ball up with the wrists is another detrimental action in the short-game swing

to get under a golf ball (with the one exception of playing from a green-side bunker) and we don't need to scoop the ball off the ground because we are using a club which has sufficient angle on it (*loft*). This *loft* will elevate the ball at an appropriate angle without you having to help it upwards in any way (assuming a good strike is made of course!). In every shot in golf, you should only ever be thinking of propelling the ball forward towards the target and allow the loft of the club to take care of the height and trajectory.

There are three vitally important aspects of the short game technique.

1. The set-up position is crucial to consistent success.

2. The club must strike the ball with a slightly descending blow and a square (or open) clubface.

3. Your rhythm must be constant and smoothly accelerating.

There are other important factors, of course, but get these three cracked and you will be more than halfway there. Let's deal with each one in turn.

7.6 Short Game Set Up Position

In order to deliver a slightly descending blow to the golf ball, you must stand with the ball positioned directly opposite the middle of you. Your upper

sternum is a good guide and represents the centre of your golf swing (known as the swing centre). If you then place slightly more weight onto your front foot (the target-side foot) you will reposition your *swing centre* so that it's slightly ahead of the ball. I call this *'lean towards the green'* as everything, including the angle of the golf club shaft, should be inclined slightly forward towards the target.

A good set-up position is vital for a good short-game swing

Therefore, as the centre of your stance and swing is the most likely place for the club to strike the ground, this ball position will make hitting the ball before the ground more likely. And yes, we do need to hit the ground, as we should on all golf shots that are struck with an iron off the fairway, rough or fringe around the green ... a perfect strike is virtually impossible otherwise.

Your stance and posture should be more akin to the way you stand to putt (or should stand to putt ... see chapter 8). You don't need a wide stance and you should be nearer to the ball and bent slightly more over it than you would normally be if using the same club for your full-power swing. Your feet should be a comfortable width apart (inside shoulder width for sure) and a line drawn across your toes should be parallel with your target line ... as should your knees, hips and shoulders. You should avoid standing *open* (chest-on) to the target (despite some coaching suggesting this) as this will encourage an across the line swing-path; standing this way will require you to make unnecessary swing compensations to produce a satisfactory result. As your pitching swing gets longer (for longer approach shots) it may help you to retract your front foot slightly from the parallel line (so only your feet and hips are *open*) in order to help you follow through more efficiently. However, you must keep your shoulders parallel with the target line to ensure your swing path is straight towards the target (NB: your shoulders in the set-up have the most influence on the path your club traces through impact with the ball).

To recap, the set-up position for all short-game shots is crucial. The ball should be positioned in the middle of your stance and equidistant from either foot. Your weight should favour your target-side foot and the club's shaft should be leaning slightly forward in order to encourage a steeper angle of approach into impact with the ball (*'lean towards the green'*). Your shoulders should align exactly parallel with your ball-to-target-line, although your front foot and front hip can be set back a little to encourage a smooth and full follow through. Practise moving into this position over and over until it becomes comfortable and repeatable ... it will then become automatic when you play on the course.

7.7 The Magic Triangle

If you set up correctly, as outlined above, much of the rest will take care of itself ... though not entirely of course as you still need to move the club ... but how?

The 'Magic triangle' for your short-game swing

As explained earlier, it is almost instinctive to get into bad habits with your short-game swing. The desire to lift or scoop the ball up is a natural one, but this encourages a swing approach which is too shallow into impact with the ball and headed upward through the strike ... a sure-fire way of hitting your shots *'thin'* or *'fat'*. It sounds obvious, but we must hit the ball before the ground and if your swing angle is too shallow you will, more than likely, hit the ground before the ball or if you're lucky enough not to hit the ground your club will be ascending into the middle of the ball causing it to fly way too low ... hitting it *thin*.

The *'Magic Triangle'* is a term I came up with to help my students visualise the ideal short-game swing technique and avoid many of the common errors highlighted above. With the correct set-up, you will be standing opposite your golf ball with the ball in the middle of your stance and your club inclined slightly towards your target. Your arms should hang straight down and there will be a relatively straight line from your target-side shoulder through the club shaft to the ball (look in a mirror). This position will create a triangle when lines are drawn across your shoulders and down each arm ... this is my 'magic triangle'. There are two ways you should evolve your swing from here, depending on where your game and technique is right now.

If you are a relative newcomer to golf you will undoubtedly be struggling with this part of the game. The nearer you get to the hole the more inconsistent you seem to be and are taking at least two, three or four shots more than you feel you should from close range. If this describes you then start with the introductory version. If you are more experienced but would still like to improve from within 50-60yds of the green, you may be ready for the more advanced short-game technique described in chapter 7.9. You may almost be there with your technique but double-check the introductory description below and move on only when you feel ready.

7.8 Your introductory short-game swing

The main principle of this swing technique is to keep the shape of the *Magic Triangle* throughout the swing. Once you have set up correctly, in the *triangle* position, all you need to do is move the triangle backwards and forwards (i.e. away from, and back towards, the target). Focus on maintaining the shape you started with. The relationship between the triangle and the golf club extending out of it should be maintained throughout the swing. There should be a conscious restriction of movement and a passiveness in your forearms and wrists throughout your swing. Any rotation in wrists or forearms will affect both the angle of the club's approach to the ball and the angle of the clubface at impact.

If you can adopt these basic principles, there will be very little to go wrong with the strike on the ball,

and it is the strike on the ball which is the key factor in distance control. Once you can achieve this consistency in ball-striking you will very quickly build up a *feel* for the right length of swing for each distance you want the ball to roll, bounce or fly. It is this appropriate length of swing that is responsible for applying the correct amount of power to the shot (and not how hard you hit at the ball).

Maintain the 'Magic Triangle' throughout the swing

To begin with, try this on very short shots, perhaps just 15 – 25 yards from the hole, using a number seven-iron. Keep your rhythm smooth and let the swing *collect* the ball as the club continues towards the target. This is crucial to the control and consistency of the shot. Like all other golf shots, we should never hit AT the ball but swing THROUGH the ball to the finish. On these shorter shots, your finish position may not be very full (maybe waist high at most) but it should always be longer than your backswing ... thus ensuring that your club is accelerating as it passes through the ball. This acceleration must be smooth and crisp, however, not jerky or rushed, and the *triangle* must keep moving in unison with the club. A common mistake is to stop your swing near the ball causing a rapid deceleration in the club-head; usually resulting in either, a duffed *fat* shot, or a duffed *thinned* shot.

You should feel that your swing simply COLLECTS the ball and not that you HIT the ball to the target. The old cliché that '*the ball merely gets in the way of your swing'* is never more appropriate than here in your short game shots.

Your worst 'enemies', in any short-game swing, are your hands. Your hands are holding the club, of course, but they shouldn't be doing any of the work. We do *feel* through our hands and fingers, but they must not be active during the swing ... they should be inactive and passive throughout.

However, this is not an instinctive thing to achieve. Instinctively, you will want to *HIT* the ball with your hands and wrists. You will be trying to lift or scoop the ball up into the air and your hands will, therefore, be over-active with this technique. So, how do we overcome this natural phenomenon?

Firstly, be aware of how your swing feels when you are not hitting the ball (i.e. during your practise swing). You are not actually hitting anything in your practise swing so your swing is more likely to be smooth. There will be a follow through and there will be a gradual acceleration of the club-head backwards and forwards. The inability to apply the same swing whilst striking the ball is a common one. It is really more of a mental problem as your mind will play tricks on you and make you doubt what you're trying to do ... precisely at the wrong moment. Your conscious mind will fear the result and, in panic, will end up adding, or taking away, something that isn't necessary, in a desperate attempt to FORCE a successful shot. Part of the problem, at least, is caused by simply looking at, and concentrating on, the ball. You are seeing the ball with your eyes, but, as the ball is not moving, your brain will contrive to hit AT the thing you are looking at. Therefore, as a practise drill, take your eyes out of the equation and play some shots with your eyes closed. This will feel odd at first (and probably a little scary), but you will learn to trust your swing as the only swing you can use is the one you *feel* and not the one that contrives to hit AT the ball. This is a useful exercise in all golf shots as the feel from your golf swing comes from inside you and not from a series of visual and mental calculations.

Once you have mastered these shorter shots with your number seven-iron, progress to a pitching wedge, sand wedge or lob wedge. You won't often need these clubs from this close to the flag but note how the trajectory of the ball flight changes for each of the clubs. Also note how much more, or less, the ball rolls when it lands. Gradually move further away from the hole and again use a variety of clubs so you can appreciate the differences in trajectory and roll.

Remember, the simpler the shot you select, the greater your chances of success. You rarely need a high shot from close to the green, but observe many club players from close range and they will probably have their shiny new lob-wedge in their hands. It may look and feel satisfying when you successfully execute the high lob-shot, but you are generally reducing your chances of success and attempting a shot which, usually, isn't necessary. Watch very good players and the pros on TV; they will always choose the safest route to the flag with the minimum of heroics. Of course, when the situation calls for a spectacular *lob-shot* they can, and will play the shot. You don't have to attempt the impossible, however, as you have a few shots to play with (i.e. your handicap) and attempting a heroic recovery shot could get you into far more trouble than you might already be in. Having said this, I know you're going to want to try the spectacular *lob-shot* nevertheless, so I had better, at least, explain how you should play it ... see later in this chapter.

Always use this adage (as described above) when close to the green: putt ... if you can putt, pitch and run (with a seven or eight-iron) ... if you can't putt, pitch and run (with a pitching wedge) if you need to fly over something but still have room for the ball to land and roll up to the flag, and only think high, or lob, if you absolutely have to (and only then if you have practised it sufficiently and have a pretty high success rate!)

7.9 Your more advanced short-game swing

In essence, there really isn't an advanced version at all. The only difference from the basic technique is that you will learn to 'see' the shot more accurately before you play it and your technique will soften slightly from the very rigid robotic technique described initially. You can relax a little on the mechanical stiffness of the 'magic triangle' technique and allow your wrists to be a little more fluid throughout the swing ... this will help you to 'feel' the shot more deftly. It is vital, however, that the club-head remains square to the target through and beyond impact and that the club is accelerating smoothly as it does so. The absolute fundamentals of your short-game swing will never change, but you can begin to add a little more depth to your thinking and process, as follows:

1. The length of swing, 'married' to a consistent rhythm, should dictate how far the ball travels (not how hard you HIT the ball).
2. Your hands must remain passive throughout the swing without manipulating the clubface in any conscious way.
3. Your legs, hips, body, shoulders and arms should swing the club ... not your hands or wrists on their own.
4. Your follow through must be longer than your backswing to ensure the club is accelerating.
5. There should be no additional HIT power through the striking zone with the ball.
6. You must hold your initial posture throughout the swing and well beyond impact with the ball. Any early move out of posture will damage your ball-striking consistency.

It is also very common for the forearms to roll over causing the clubface to close through the striking area

7. Hold the finish position and watch everything about the flight of the ball, sensing exactly how the swing and strike felt in executing the shot. If successful, lock the feeling in for next time. If unsuccessful, feel what went wrong. Was it the strike on the ball? Was there too much or

insufficient power? Did you misjudge the landing area or forget to 'read' the green? Did you get a lucky or an unlucky bounce? Soak all this information in for every shot you play and your 'feel' will improve gradually (there is no suddenly) the more you play.

7.10 The lob shot

This is one of the most overplayed shots in the game. The true lob shot requires that you lay the clubface of your lob wedge almost flat with the ground and make a full swing, with a lot of power, that slides the club-head perfectly underneath the ball with absolutely no margin for error in striking the ball ... no wonder this shot is also known as 'the suicide lob'!

The simplest way to get the ball higher is to use the technique you have become comfortable with (as described in the previous pages), but open the clubface when setting up to the ball. You should align your set-up a little in the opposite direction to offset the clubface angle and then use your new short-game swing as you have practised already. The same swing, combined with the open clubface, will automatically send the ball higher and allow it to land more softly on the green. Either way, be selective with this choice of shot and use it sparingly ... you will very rarely need it in all honesty.

7.11 Visualise your shots

Once you have practised and become comfortable with your new short-game swing, you will be better equipped to become more accurate with your control of distance for each type of shot. With each successful shot you will build up a memory bank of good habits and good results which you can call upon when you feel under pressure during a game. You will begin to use your imagination more effectively and more easily visualise how the ball will fly and react when it lands; you will begin to 'see' the shot in your 'mind's eye' before you play it.

It is this ability to visualise the shot that will really sharpen up your short game. You will start to ask yourself 'where do I need to land the ball, in order for it to roll up to the hole'? 'What are the contours of the green'? 'What will happen to my ball when it lands on the green'? 'Will it land on an upslope or down-slope'? 'Will it 'kick' left or right if landing on a side-slope'? You may feel, at this stage, that this depth of thinking is too advanced, or that only better players think this way, but if you practise sufficiently you will soon acquire the confidence to believe in the shot and begin to think this specifically. Besides, thinking positively about the outcome of any golf shot is a big step towards executing it successfully (see chapter 9 on the mental game).

Once you can fully visualise the shot at hand you will have a better understanding of the club you need to execute the shot. There are three basic short-game shots to visualise.

1. If there is a hazard-free path between your ball and the flag, and the grass is dry and short in between, you could simply play a low running shot with a six-iron, seven-iron, or an eight-iron. This is generally the safest and most pressure-resistant shot to play. This is the pitch-and-run shot (or 'bump-and-run' as it is also known). There isn't a precise landing area for this shot as the ball will barely get airborne and will start rolling after a few 'bumpy' bounces. You should judge the distance of the bump and run by imagining the force you would require if you were putting from the same distance, but add a little more power. This is because the ball will have backspin on it (caused by the grooves and loft of the club) and will 'check' slightly as it bounces.

2. If you need to land the ball on the green because there is a hazard in the way, or you are playing over rough, then a more lofted shot will be required. However, you should still work with the available part of the green and imagine your ball bouncing and then rolling up to the target. You will play this shot with a pitching wedge or a gap wedge. Still imagine a pitch and run, however, but with a slightly higher ball flight … a kind of half-fly, half-roll kind of shot.

3. You should only think of playing a super-high-flying shot when there is very little available green between you and the flag, or you have to fly directly over a hazard or long grass. Using a club with a large amount of loft (i.e. a sand

wedge or lob wedge) increases the difficulty of the shot and the strike needs to be much more precise and, therefore, the risk of failure is greater. Be sparing with the frequency that you play this shot, but even if you feel you have to play it, you can still play it with a degree of caution. If the only way of getting close to the flag is to land the ball a few inches beyond the hazard in front of you, then maybe the risk is too high. You should recognise that you are in trouble and accept that a shot ending a little bit past the hole is acceptable and maybe the best you can safely achieve. If you learn to have faith in your putting, you will be less compelled to risk an overly-ambitious shot.

7.12 Appropriate length of swing

So, we have evaluated the situation and imagined the shot we need to play. All that is needed now is to find the required amount of club-head speed to propel the ball to the landing point we have visualised. However, if we can't simply hit harder or softer (as suggested earlier), how do we control the length of each shot? The answer lies with the variation in length of swing you make and swinging with a consistently smooth rhythm. By varying the swing length, we can feel that we are swinging at the same rhythm for each distance we play from. The obvious next question is, therefore, how do we find the correct length of swing for the shot we are about to play?

You will find this with practise, of course, but you need to practise in the right way and develop the feel for just the right swing and also a strategy to help you retain that feel when you play on the course.

There are many methods you could come up with yourself to help you gauge the distance accurately, but I will suggest a few which may give you a head start. The most important thing, as with all golf shots, is that you SWING and don't HIT. You must simply let the ball get in the way of an appropriately powered swing (i.e. an appropriate length of swing) for the shot at hand. You must keep your hands and wrists 'passive' throughout the swing and yet the club-head must be smoothly accelerating through impact.

But, how do we create a smoothly accelerating swing, which simply 'collects' the ball as it goes? Also, and just as importantly, how do you control the distance the ball flies or rolls? The follow through must be longer than the backswing for sure … this takes care of the acceleration part … and if you swing with a smooth tempo and make a longer forward-swing than backswing the club will be accelerating through impact. This being the case, if we can find a way to gauge the backswing length in some measurable way, we're 'in business.' Here are some options to help you 'measure' just the right amount of swing.

7.12.1 Percentage of your full swing

If your full swing (your power swing) represents 100% of your backswing, you could shorten your swing by percentage points as appropriate to the distance and club you have in your hand. Start with obvious backswing percentages like 75%, 50%, 25%, etc. and note how far the ball travels with each of your short game clubs (nine-iron, pitching-wedge, sand-wedge and lob-wedge). Remember, however, that the follow through should always be longer than the backswing, so add a higher percentage onto the follow through. As a general rule, add 25% onto the follow through compared to the backswing length. For example: 75% backswing = 100% follow through. 50% backswing = 75% follow through. 25% backswing = 50% follow through.

Use this equation for all of your short-game clubs and you will soon associate a yardage, with a certain percentage of backswing/follow through for each club. Thus, if you have four short-game clubs, and they each have three backswing lengths, you already have twelve distances covered.

7.12.2 Fractions

You may prefer to think of your backswing in terms of fractions of your full swing rather than percentages. You may find it easier to think in terms such as; full swing, three-quarter swing, half swing, quarter swing, etc. The results will be the same as above (i.e. percentages) if you apply the same thinking to the follow through. For example; ¾ backswing=full follow through, ½ backswing=¾ follow through, ¼ backswing=½ follow through, and so on.

7.12.3 Clock face

Another commonly adopted system is to think about your backswing length associated with the hour hands of a clock. With an imaginary clock-face behind you, the position of your arms in the backswing can relate to a certain O'CLOCK position … your arms in the backswing, for example, may point to a seven o'clock position on our imaginary clock face. You must ensure, however, that you swing to the corresponding time in the follow through … plus one hour. Consequently, you will have a longer follow through than backswing and a smoothly accelerating club head. In the following example, this 3:30 follow through position would have used a 7:30 backswing position. See diagram overleaf.

Your target-side arm should represent the backswing o'clock position and the other arm your follow through 'time'.

Other examples: -
- 7 o'clock backswing = 4 o'clock follow through
- 8 o'clock backswing = 3 o'clock follow through
- 8.30 backswing = 2.30 follow through
- 9 = 2, 10 = 1, etc., etc.

Each backswing length will correspond to a certain yardage using clubs of differing lengths and lofts. Each swing will propel the ball forward, landing a certain distance away from you. Make a note of these distances and take your notes with you when you play and practise. Some players even tape the distances for each swing length onto their wedges (perfectly within the rules) so they have a reference every time they play.

7.12.4 Summary of systems

Whichever system you choose, with regular practise, you will soon build up a feel for multiple backswing lengths with each of your main short-game clubs. Combine these backswings with the corresponding length of follow through, whilst keeping a consistent rhythm, and ultimately you will acquire a repertoire of distances with each of these clubs.

7.13 Upon Landing

We also need to acquire a good understanding of what our ball is likely to do when it lands. Will it stop? Will it shoot forward? Will it 'kick' sideways? There are multiple factors involved here, but the most influential ones are pureness of strike, the trajectory of the ball, and the construction of the ball itself.

Acknowledging your strike on the ball (pureness of strike) is important in strengthening your feel for the distance. If you strike the ball too low on the clubface (thin) the ball will fly much lower and land sooner than you had anticipated. Neither will it have much backspin imparted upon it and, on landing, will shoot forward more than you predicted. You will feel a significant vibration through your fingers when you contact the ball in this way. If we hit the ball too high on the clubface it is usually because we have struck the ground before the ball ... a 'fat' contact. How far the ball flies is very much down to how 'fat' we hit the ball. If you strike the ground considerably behind your ball, you may not hit the ball at all and it might only fly a few feet in front of you. If the ground is struck only fractionally before the ball, the end result may not be too dissimilar from what you expected. The ball may also be struck slightly towards the heel of the club, or the toe of the club, but this will have a minimal effect on the result ... not from close range at least.

The trajectory of the ball-flight (assuming a pure strike) is, thereafter, dictated entirely by the loft of the club you are using. A number seven-iron with a short swing, for example, will barely get the ball airborne at all and there won't really be a specific landing area as such. This is more of a 'bobbling' kind of shot, hence its other common name ... 'bump and run.' A pitching wedge, on the other hand, will fly a little higher and you can begin to imagine your landing point ... but still allow for a significant amount of bounce and roll. The higher lofted wedges, such as, your sand-wedge and lob-wedge should send the ball much higher and there will be significantly less roll upon landing. Please note, however, that a higher-flying ball will be more susceptible to 'kicking' sideways if it lands on a slope.

The type of ball you use can also make a significant difference to the result of a shot. Balls vary hugely, not just from manufacturer to manufacturer, but also within the same maker's range of balls. Some are very hard and they all have varying spin-rates. Some have very little sophisticated technology within their structure, whilst others are designed with the very best of players in mind. In short, some balls stop quicker than others and some balls spring off the clubface more than you might expect. Experiment with different types of ball and also ask your local golf professional for advice on which type of ball is best suited to your game. Once you have decided on a particular brand and type, stick with it: a certain route to inconsistency is to use a different kind of ball on every hole!

Fully understanding how your ball is likely to behave upon landing is mostly down to experience. However, the more you understand the influences of ball construction, ground conditions, pureness of strike, etc. and the more you take note of the feel and result of every shot, the better you will be able to predict the consequences of each shot you play. Practise in realistic situations by moving around the practise green ... playing one shot at a time ... instead of playing from one spot continuously. You can practise your technique in this way, but it is not so good for strengthening your feel for distance and control.

7.14 Judgement of Distance

Of course, none of the above is of any use unless you know how far away you are from your chosen landing area. I would recommend you purchase an optical distance measuring device so that you will always know, within a yard, how far you have to any chosen point. A GPS-type device has its merits, but, unless very expensive, its screen will only show hazards (that you can probably see anyway) and indicate how far you have to the middle of the green. I hasten to add, the middle of the green is never a bad place to be but, as you progress, you will aspire to become more accurate than this. An optical device can be directed at any object, including: the front or back edge of the green, the far edge of a bunker/water hazard, a tree or a bank in front of the green and, of course, your chosen landing zone or the flag itself. If you also use this device when you practise you can very quickly build an accurate memory bank of distances related to lengths of swing. And it is this memory bank of successful shots that you will need to call upon when you are on the course.

You can also become a good judge of distance without any mechanical devices. After all, the great players of old didn't have this kind of help and even the top players today can't use these devices in actual play (although they do have extremely accurate yardage maps, prepared by specialist companies, so they do always know within a foot, or so, how far they have to go). If you practise, effectively, from known distances and you can 'marry' the right length of swing to that distance with the particular club you have in your hand, you are well on your way. We are always guessing the right swing length for the appropriate shot, but, the more we practise, the better we get at guessing!

Once you are comfortable with the concepts described above you will need to incorporate them into a solid routine that will help you execute successful shots on the course. This process is the same in putting and is described in detail in the following chapter.

A significant proportion of this book has been dedicated to the short-game and putting, for the simple reason that, whatever your ability or handicap, the majority of your shots during a round of golf will comprise short pitches, low pitches, high pitches, long pitches, bunkers shots or putts. I will wager that 70% of all your shots are played from within 70 – 80 yards of the hole. I also wager that you don't spend 70% of your practise time on these shots! We all want to hit the ball impressively from the tee, and from the fairway to the green, but become a proficient player from inside these distances and your game will be a match for anyone!

CHAPTER 8

Putting

8.1 The game within the game

You've probably heard this expression before, but putting truly is, 'the game within the game'. That is to say, that becoming a good putter (or remaining a poor one) has nothing to do with your physical prowess at 'striping' the ball down the fairway or onto the green. Indeed, children often make the best putters as they have a wonderful ability to see only the job at hand ... without worrying about the final result.

Putting ... the 'game within the game!'

Putting could almost be described as an art-form, rather than a sport, and some people are naturally more adept at this skill than others. However, improving your putting skill can be achieved relatively easily and quickly if you learn some fundamental good habits.

Becoming a good putter is not about holing all your putts. It's about reducing the total number of putts you take in a round of golf (which you should always record). Even the best of putters, on the professional tours, average nearer to two putts per green than one (around 1.6 putts per green at best) ... therefore, even the best of players miss over half of their first putts.

A good putter, however, is never very far from the hole after their first putt. Having expertly judged the speed and contours of the green, the better putter leaves their ball within two or three feet of the hole more often than not. It is with improved control of direction and distance that you will learn to become a better putter.

During this chapter, we will discuss the skills required to improve your putting which primarily comprise:

1. Accurately 'reading' the contours and elevation changes of the green.
2. The technique that will ensure your ball starts rolling in the right direction.
3. The 'feel' required to roll your ball the correct speed for the distance and 'shape' of your putt.

Putting is generally considered least, in order of skill-level required, amongst new players. However, talk to many experienced players and they will tell you how important a skill it is and how costly it can be to your score if you are not reasonably proficient. Unfortunately, the rules of the game dictate that a six-foot putt counts the same as your best drive from the tee.

I say 'six-foot putt' because most players, on average, will miss more of these than they make (especially new players), but even new players don't miss many two-foot putts. Therefore, the prime prerequisite of better putting is to ensure most of your putts end within two feet of the hole ... as, otherwise, the statistics suggest that you are more likely to miss the next one. Your first putt on each green is, therefore, of prime importance. If you regularly leave your first putt more than a couple of feet away from the hole you will take three putts, or more, far too often.

8.2 Reading the green

The ability to 'read' the green, before you putt, is not a mythical gift from the golfing gods, it is a skill that can be acquired. It is primary, however, in the process of getting your ball close to the hole from long range and into the hole from short range.

You should always start from the premise that your putt is not straight and the green is not flat (if you subsequently decide after careful evaluation that it is then that's ok).

Reading the green is paramount to becoming a better putter!

Reading any green, accurately, is based upon the accumulated knowledge you have gained from previous successes and mistakes. You must watch every putt, to its very end, to fully understand whether you interpreted the contours of the green correctly. Do not be annoyed or despondent if you completely misread a putt ... just learn from it. Reading greens

well requires experience ... a back-catalogue of successes and failures if you like ... but the more you learn and practise, the closer your failures will be.

So, how do we set about reading the greens? There is no clever secret. There are no witch-doctors involved and you don't need to be an expert in turf maintenance to become good at it. Understanding how your ball rolls along the green is simply down to an

The best vantage point from which to view your putt ... the lower the better!

acquired knowledge founded from careful observation over a period of time. The most important thing of all is that you actually DO IT on every

putt you attempt. This doesn't mean that all your putts will always drop in the hole, but they might just have more of a fighting chance.

When observing many new clients, I see little or no preparation when they putt. There might be a cursory glance at the 'lie of the land', but rarely from the right position. Not looking at the contours of the green before you putt is akin to setting out on a journey to a destination you have never been to before without turning on your Sat-nav or looking at a map. You might set off vaguely in the right direction and you will get there eventually ... but it will have taken a lot longer than it could have. If you don't get into the habit of reading your putts, you will be lucky to hole any of them ... and we don't want to rely on luck.

Let's break down the process into stages. Watch the best players on TV whenever you get the chance and observe this process. It sounds long-winded when you write it down but, with experience, you will absorb all the relevant factors for any putt in just a few seconds.

Firstly, what is going to affect the speed of the putt? Is it significantly downhill or uphill? Is the grass wet or dry? Has the grass just been cut, or is it later in the day? (Throughout the day the grass will grow sufficiently to alter the speed of the green). Is the wind behind the line of your putt, or against? (a significant wind will definitely affect the speed of your putt). Even the direction that the grass leans towards (the grain) will affect the speed of your putt (although you will already be a pretty good putter before you concern yourself too much with this kind of detail). Combine two, three, or more of these factors and you will begin to understand the complexities in judging the correct speed for each putt. For example, a downhill putt on a freshly cut green, with the wind behind, might require the barest of touches with the putter. Whereas, a putt of the same distance coming the opposite way will require a substantial strike by comparison.

Secondly, is there any slope across the line of your putt? Or, perhaps, two or more opposing slopes? If so, your ball will curve as it makes its journey across the green. How much it will curve is directly linked to the severity of the slope and the speed your ball will be travelling at; the slower the ball is rolling, the more it will curve. Therefore, a pronounced downhill putt with a curve will curve significantly more than a steep uphill putt as there will be more time for the forces of gravity to affect the ball.

At this stage, it would also be useful to acquire some knowledge of the terminology used to describe the curve of your ball on the green. Listen to the TV commentators describing the putt a player is about to face. They will use terms such as 'break'; meaning how much the ball will 'break' away to the left or right as it rolls. They may describe the putt as having a right-to-left 'borrow' or, conversely, a left-to-right borrow. This means that the player has to borrow a certain amount of the slope in order for the putt to curve (or break) towards the hole. How much the putt may curve, or break, or how much you may have to borrow is usually described in feet or inches or 'cup' (hole) widths to one side or the other. On shorter, or almost straight putts, your aim point could be described as half a cup to the right or, perhaps, 'a ball width outside the left' or, 'just inside the right lip' (the lip being the left or right edge of the hole as you look at it). Whatever you choose to call the curve of your putt, these terms are used to establish your 'aim-point' ... the direction your ball should initially start off in. Your aim-point could be something in the distance; a tree or the rake in a nearby bunker for example. Your aim-point could simply be a different coloured patch on the green near to, or on the way to the hole, or even a tiny scratch on the inside of the hole that fits with your 'read' of the putt. Establishing your aim-point takes experience and is always an educated guess, but the more you play and practise the more likely it is that your guess will be correct. The most important factor in this part of the process is that you TRUST your 'read' and, even if it turns out to be wrong, you take a few moments to understand why.

With time, you may well become extremely proficient at reading all your putts, but as the amount of curve is directly linked to the speed of the ball as it rolls, you will need to further explore this relationship and understand the third stage of the putting process ... feel (explained in 8.5).

8.3 All putts are straight

Before we explore 'feel', we need to learn the technique that will help set the ball rolling in the direction we have chosen and at approximately the right speed. I say approximately the right speed as there is no way of knowing for sure what the right speed is. Rolling the ball at the correct speed is not an exact science. How fast you set the ball in motion represents your best guess and experience helps you get better at guessing.

We can, however, use a more scientific approach to ensure the ball at least starts off in the right direction. For the ball to start rolling exactly towards the target you have chosen depends on two major factors. Firstly, that the ball is struck from the middle of the clubface and, secondly, that the clubface is exactly ninety degrees (right angles) to your chosen target. I say 'chosen target' as the target is not always the hole itself due to the likelihood of your putt curving (especially on longer putts). However, having said this, I want you to understand that all putts are straight ... at least as far as your ball and putter is concerned.

Your 'reading of the green' will have established the slope of the ground between your ball and the hole. It is likely that this will involve starting your ball rolling at a target that is not the hole but at your aim-point ... which will be inches or feet to either the left or right of the hole. Your ball will, therefore, need to start rolling at your aim-point (with the correct speed of course) in order for the putt to be successful. However, the line between your ball and aim-point is always straight, so we are, therefore, always putting along a straight line ... so, we don't actually need to practise curved putts at all!

This concept may seem quite obvious. However, I put it this way because I see so many people aiming at the hole (even though they know the ball will curve) and manipulating their putting stroke to force the ball to start left or right of the hole. Thus, if all putts are straight, all we need to do is practise putting along a straight line ... sounds easy, doesn't it? However, nothing in golf is that easy or it wouldn't be the challenge that it is.

8.4 Putting set-up and technique

There is much argument, even amongst seasoned players and coaches, surrounding the ideal swing path the putter should take as it passes through the ball. The alternatives being; either a slightly curved stroke, or one that swings straight back and straight through. Many great players have putted successfully with either method, but I prefer my players to learn a stroke that is as straight as possible as it is the most logical for you to learn and the easiest to practise.

You must not, however, get obsessed with making the putter swing exactly straight as it will take the emphasis away from the other, more important, factors in putting such as, feel and distance control. The crucial thing, for accuracy, is that your putter follows through straight towards your chosen target for at least an inch or two after impact. Provided that your backswing is relatively straight you will, therefore, have a straight back and through putting stroke. You can practise this by swinging your putter over a known straight line, such as the grout line of kitchen tiles, or the edges of floorboards, or over the top of another golf club that you have placed on the floor.

8.4.1 Set-up

Let's focus now on the set-up position and swing technique that is most likely to allow this to happen.

First of all, we need to get everything square to, and square with, the target line. Your putter should start at an exact right angle (90°) to your target. You should then stand so that you are exactly parallel with your target line (see pictures).

Set up to the ball with feet aligned parallel to your target-line with your eyes over the ball

Your eyes should be directly over the ball, which helps you to see along the target line more easily. You should bend slightly forward from your hips and let your arms hang straight downwards.

From this position, your arms will be able to swing from your shoulders and create a pendulum action when you swing. This is more likely to create a straight-backwards and straight-forwards stroke when you putt. It is crucial, therefore, that your putter is the correct length to fit with this set up. You should never adapt your set-up to accommodate the length of a standard putter; always have it made or altered to be the correct length for YOU. Your Club's professional will help you with this.

Your ball should be positioned slightly forward of middle (of your stance)

123

8.4.2 Grip

As you can plainly see by watching the best players on the professional tour, there are many ways of holding a putter successfully. However, there are a few common factors which are important in helping you to putt more accurately and with more feel for the distance.

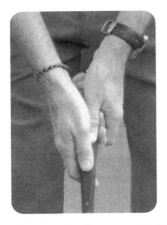

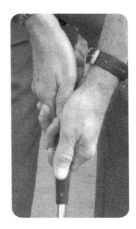

The conventional 'reverse overlap' grip (right-hander shown)

The ever more popular cross-handed putting grip (right-hander shown)

The pictures above show the conventional 'reverse overlap' grip (left) and the less conventional cross-handed grip ... very much used in the modern game. This 'hands the wrong way around' approach to holding the club does have some logical advantages and many top players do adopt similar methods. In your power-swing grip your 'natural' hand is likely to be at the bottom and this will add raw power to your full swing. This, however, is very much unwanted in your putting stroke. There are dozens of tiny variations within these two most common grips and literally scores of other weird and wacky interpretations. I wouldn't deviate too much, however, from the conventional grip until you have mastered the many other challenges in putting.

Whichever grip you adopt, unlike your power-swing grip as described in chapter five, you should hold your putter much more in the palm of your hand (note the watch-face is not visible as opposed to the tip given for the full swing grip). This is primarily because we do not want to use our hands actively in the putting stroke. Our hands are created with many small muscles and ligaments and these are the 'little devils' that can cause the twitches and the *'yips'*. If you wrap your fingers around the grip too much your hands are likely to be over-active throughout your putting swing.

You should also hold your putter quite lightly and, above all, ensure that your hands stay passive and in-active throughout your stroke. Your putting feel and swing should come from your shoulders and arms and definitely not from your hands and wrists.

8.4.3 Your putting swing (stroke)

Once you have adopted the ideal grip, stance, posture and alignment and you are using a putter of the correct length, we can begin to practise the best swing technique so that delivery of the putter head is consistently square to the target and swinging along a straight line through impact.

At first, you can practise this putting swing (or 'stroke' as we refer to it) without using your putter. Stand in your putting posture with your arms hanging straight down from your shoulders (use a mirror to check this). Now bring your hands together and place them palm to palm. From this position, swing your arms back and forth and feel that they swing freely from your shoulder joints. This will create an almost perfect pendulum swing that goes straight back and straight through (similar to the 'magic triangle' as explained in the previous chapter). Feel that the forward swing (follow through) is longer than the backswing ... this will ensure a smooth acceleration. The rest of your body and head should stay as still as possible. Again, use a mirror to check that you stay still or your use your shadow if you practise with your back to the sun.

Once you have repeatedly practised this action you can add the final piece of the jigsaw. You must ensure your hands, forearms and wrists remain completely passive through impact with the ball. This is quite straightforward without the ball, but when we are playing the shot our hands tend to take over and unnecessarily manipulate the putter as we strike the ball (this is how the *yips* develop). We, therefore, need to make a conscious effort to keep everything passive throughout the stoke. There shouldn't be any particular 'hit' point and the ball should merely get in the way of the stroke ... the length of the stroke determining how far the ball will roll. Finally, you should hold the finish and, preferably, without looking up until the ball is well on its way to the target. Swing back and swing through ... swing your arms from your shoulders without any manipulation by your hands and wrists and you will become a much better putter very quickly.

8.4.4 The finish

Like every other shot in the game, you should hold your finish! Finish the stroke and don't look up until the ball is well on its way (on short putts you should listen for the ball dropping into the hole and not look  up until then). On longer putts, you can look up once the stroke is finished but don't come up out of your posture. From this position, watch everything that the ball does and let every detail 'soak' into your memory. Did the ball do everything you had envisaged, or were you surprised by the result? Either way, this is how we learn for future reference.

8.4.5 Where next?

Now you have learned to 'read' the green and have acquired and practised a solid putting stroke, you are ready to start bringing the whole thing together. Your new-found technique and green-reading wizardly now need the chemistry to meld everything together. You will need to 'feel' your putting stroke in relation to the length of putt, the speed of the green and the contours of the ground.

8.5 But, what is ... feel?

Feel is our uniquely personal ability to sense or perceive something that can't be measured in any conventional way. Feel is not a mathematical thing, or a logical thing; it's a sensory, biological, almost emotional thing. In golf (especially in putting and the short game), your sense of feel helps you judge the speed, or power, you need to successfully execute the shot. It helps you perceive (we can never know for sure) just the right amount of swing necessary to propel the ball at the appropriate speed and to sense the line your ball should be rolling on. Although an innate ability, your golfing *feel* needs to be learned. Your feel is a gift and is acquired over a relatively long period of time ... made up from the memories of our successes ... but also from our failures. Yes, do not ignore your failures and never turn away from a misjudged putt (or pitch) as you will always learn something from what went wrong. Did you misread the line? Did you hit the ball too softly or too hard? Did you strike the ball from anywhere but the sweet spot of your putter? Always take a few moments to analyse what went wrong and lock it away in your memory bank. After all, if you think about it objectively, golf is a game of mistakes as very few shots succeed exactly as we would have wished ... though we have to deal with the result nonetheless. Therefore, our continuous journey towards improved performance is not about striving for perfection, but about learning from our *mistakes* and ensuring our misses are not too penalising.

To emphasise, once again, even the best players miss most of their first putts, but they don't miss by much and there always seems to be the possibility that the ball might just drop in to the hole. Great players also hit poor shots from the tee and fairway as well, but their misses are usually manageable and recoverable with minimal effect on their score. The important lesson is that we must always learn from these mistakes (especially where putting is concerned) and build a mental library of how we can do things better in the future.

Feel, however, cannot be directly passed from coach to pupil as everyone's feel is uniquely their own. It is not a transferable skill, but it can be acquired and enhanced with trust and faith in our natural instincts. Practise and technique, alone, do not make up the whole story ... you need to develop your golfing 'sixth sense' and then learn to trust it when you play. In this book, I cannot teach you feel, but I can suggest methods of practising which help you to understand your own feel.

Your feel (or touch, as it is sometimes referred to) is your innate ability to sense or perceive things ... which we do all the time in everyday life if we choose to acknowledge it. We sense the slope we are walking along, we sense the wind in our face, we sense the texture of things and the deftness that is required to achieve a particular action or skill. In short, we are generally more naturally talented than we might otherwise equate with our golfing ability. We need to learn the physical skills of golf, but then learn to 'let them go' in order to maximise our natural sense of feel.

How do we bring this natural sense of feel into our putting? With practise, and a reasonably proficient technique, you can learn to roll the ball consistently along a straight line relatively easily. However, rolling the ball the right distance, given all the variables of slope, speed of green, wind and psychological tension, it's a wonder we can do it at all. We must, therefore, 'feel' the putt more than we 'think' it. We need to combine all the factors of slope, speed, wind etc. into a feeling we can transmit into the physical action of sending the ball on its way. You must trust your instincts and just 'let the putt go' without any fear of missing. You must convince yourself that the line you have chosen is correct and that you have an exact aim-point to start the ball rolling towards. You will, I sincerely hope, have stroked some putts on the practise green before you play and will, therefore, appreciate the speed of the greens on that day. You will also be able to feel the wind in your face, or at your back, and be able to combine all these variables into a stroke of sufficient length and power to achieve a satisfactory result.

Can you, however, just walk up to the ball and make this happen by magic? No, of course you can't, but you can rehearse the stroke you believe you need (multiple times if you wish) before you execute the actual shot … you can, in this way, rehearse the putt first.

When making your practise strokes, you should let all the relevant information *soak* through your brain and through your hands to the putter head … let everything almost 'wash over you'. Feel the wind in your face, or at your back, look at the hole and back again to the ball ... observe the slope and elevation changes along the way. Do not look down at the ground or at your putter as you make your practise swings. Doing so will make you overly conscious of the mechanics of your stroke and this is not the time to be worried about your technique. Be completely target focused. Look forward and back along your aim-line but don't get preoccupied with what your putter is doing. Better still, don't look back to your putter at all during your practise swings. This is a tricky habit to get into, but by looking only at your aim-point and the grass in between, whilst swinging your arms, will give you a very natural and accurate sense of feel for the power you need. After all, you don't look at your hand when you toss a ball to someone or toss a piece of paper into the rubbish bin ... you look at the other person ... or the bin. Neither do you look at the ball when playing Boule on the beach or bowling to the jack on a bowling green. Therefore, look at the hole when you rehearse the putt and then, without delay or second-guessing your feel, move in and stroke the ball towards your target. The more you dwell or delay over the ball the more you will lose the feel you have just rehearsed. I don't suggest you look at the hole while actually striking the ball as a clean strike from the middle of the putter face becomes less likely. However, this is a great practise drill for gaining feel and many great players have actually putted this way from time to time in order to regain the feel and trust they may have temporarily lost.

One other question I often get asked, relating to feel and distance control, is 'where should I look on putts with a significant amount of break in them?' (i.e.

should I look at the hole or look at the aim-point?'). Your aim-point can often be several feet off from the line to the hole itself and can be confusing to your eyes and brain. You will, no doubt, get different answers to this question from different coaches (and players) as there are logical answers in favour of either. I suggest you experiment with both methods as there is no right or wrong way. Personally, I like to look at the hole as it is more relevant to distance control and is, after all, the target you are endeavouring to get close to. You should still align your putter carefully at right angles to your chosen aim-point, but then look at the hole for a better feel for the distance. If you choose this method, however, you must trust your alignment and stroke the ball along your aim-line and not get influenced by your last look at the hole (as we can almost instinctively swing the putter towards the last thing we looked at).

8.6 Your Putting (and pitching) Routine

Now we have to put the three elements discussed above into practise, but without consciously thinking about them too much. You cannot think about all the components of line, technique and feel at the same time, as there are literally dozens of factors involved. You need to practise each phase of the process until you are comfortable with each one. Practise your putting set-up and technique until you can confidently roll your ball along a straight line. Understand and implement the requirements of green-reading and feel. You will now be ready to build yourself a solid and repeatable putting routine that you employ on every putt you make.

Your putting routine (as with any other golf shot) should be exactly that ... a routine ... an exactly replicated procedure that you follow each time. Your routine will need to be thought out and rehearsed again and again until it feels natural and automatic. This may take a little time, but your routine will soon become your 'crutch' and one that you can ultimately rely on under pressure when you play.

Your routine is completely of your own design, but watch better players to get a sense of how they do things. Your routine must involve the three main elements of aim, technique and feel, but without being overly mindful of any ... your routine should be one-two-three, or, as I call it ... see it, feel it, do it.

8.6.1 See it ... reading the green

Observe the contours of the green between your ball and the hole and choose your aim-point. 'See' the putt in your mind's eye and visualise the line the ball will take. Even better, visualise the ball falling into the hole.

8.6.2 Feel it ... rehearse the putt

This is not the time to be rehearsing your technique, but you need to have practise swings in order to feel the amount of swing (stroke) you need. The amount of swing, or length of swing, should be directly proportionate to the distance to the hole and the speed of the green. If you keep your rhythm consistent and simply vary the length of your putting stroke, your ball will roll different distances without the need to feel you are hitting harder or softer.

8.6.3 Do it … let the putt go

There is absolutely no point in going through any of the above if you then tense up, don't trust what you're doing, and become tentative. We could write a whole book about the mental side of golf (and there are hundreds of them … including a significant chapter in this book) but the most important word here is TRUST. You've read the green and visualised your line … you've *'seen'* it. You've rehearsed the stroke that will send the ball away at the right speed … you've *'felt'* it. You must then step up to your ball and execute without delay. It has been suggested, in scientific circles, that if you take any longer than 6-8 seconds, following your last practise stroke, you are already beginning to lose the feel from your rehearsal swing (this applies equally to all your golf shots!). Initially, this may not seem long enough for you to step up to your ball, set your stance again, and aim your putter. However, with sufficient practise and repetition you can easily perform your routine and set your ball rolling within this time frame. Take longer than this and you will lose the physical memory of the stroke you have just practised … you will also be susceptible to your mind meandering in unhelpful directions. The longer you take, the more your head will become full of thoughts that just shouldn't be there. Am I aimed straight? Is my ball-position correct? Is my head over the ball? Did I leave the gas on?! In short, the longer you take, the more you will doubt ... and the less confidently you will roll the putt.

NB: The strategy described here should also be used as the core of your routine for all your short game shots or any shot that requires feel above all else.

8.7 Rhythm in putting

The rhythm of your swing is of vital importance in all golf shots and just as important in putting. Your rhythm is your commitment to the stroke. It's your metronome and the backbone of your stroke. Your stroke should be like the pendulum of a grandfather clock swinging relentlessly backwards and forwards ... tick-tock, tick-tock. You can find your own speed of *tick-tock* but it should always be the same back and through. Be aware that the 'tick' should be at the end of the backswing and the 'tock' is at the end of follow through ... contact with the ball should happen somewhere in the middle and be inconsequential to the swing of the putter. The old adage that is ... 'let the ball get in the way of the swing'.

If you are really serious about your game, then you could measure the rhythm of your putting stroke using a metronome (purchased quite cheaply from a music shop). Experiment with differing bleep patterns until you find one that is comfortable and repeatable. If you can stick to a consistent rhythm all you then need do is vary the length of the stroke and the ball will travel different distances accordingly. Your practise swing will give you the feel and your rhythm will help you repeat it under pressure when you strike the ball. Your rhythm is your secret to distance control and, if greens were flat, you could become pin-point accurate with your control of how far the ball rolls for a given length of swing. Unfortunately, however, greens are not flat. Greens slope up and down and from side to side but you can equalise the situation, to a degree, by changing your aim-points accordingly. For instance, if your putt is downhill you can putt to an imaginary point on the green that is closer to you than the hole itself. Conversely, if the putt is uphill, you can imagine an aim-point which is somewhat beyond the hole. How much closer or how much beyond the hole you envisage is, of course, dictated by the severity of the slope and the speed of the green; experience and practise will help you learn how much to allow.

8.8 Putting Summary

Do not underestimate the challenge and importance of putting. Whatever level of golf you play at, well over a third of your score will be made up from putts. Even if you shoot in the 70's or 80's regularly over 40% of your shots will have required a putting stroke. Many great players in history have attempted to diminish the importance of putting, arguing that it is the least skilful element of the game and should not be of such significance to the result. Ben Hogan even argued that the hole should be made bigger to give the less skilful putters a chance and the rules did change for a while. However, all this achieved was to make putting much easier for the better putters and the results remained, largely, the same ... so the dimensions of the hole quickly reverted to the original size.

So, if forty percent plus of your score is comprised of *putts,* do you spend forty percent of your practise time on putting? Almost certainly not. I'm not, necessarily, suggesting you do spend forty percent of your practise time on putting, as many holes finish with simple 'tap-ins' which don't need a lot of practise. But, you should spend a significant amount of time practising your long putting, for distance control, and your short putting from six to ten feet as these are the crucial ones. Always remember, any more than an average of two putts per hole is simply a waste of your true golfing potential.

CHAPTER 9

The mental side of golf (see it, feel it, do it!)

9.1 What's the problem?

No other ball sport represents quite the mental challenge that golf does. Most other sports involve a direct opponent you can blame for a lost point and a moving ball which you can, at least, use the momentum of. In golf, you have nobody to blame but yourself. The fact that the ball is stationary means that YOU are the only reason the shot can go wrong. You can blame your out of date clubs, you can blame the wind or rain, you can blame anything you want, but, quite honestly, it's all down to you! This makes the mental challenge paramount to your golfing success as you (and me, of course) are the only One that cares about the result.

The number of times I've heard my clients say ... 'I can hit the ball beautifully on the practise range, but it all goes to pieces on the course' ... I can't begin to remember. The number of great practise swings I've witnessed that don't resemble the swing that is used to strike the ball would have to be seen to be believed. So, what makes it so hard to repeat what we've just rehearsed when we actually play the shot? The reason is that there are suddenly consequences that result from hitting the ball. You can practise-swing beautifully, all day long, but if you can't commit to the swing you have practised when you play the ball, your old habits will automatically take over.

In order to implement the good habits suggested within the pages of this book, we must be able to commit to a swing, pitch, or putt, without caring about the result ... but herein lies the problem. There is a result of some kind every time you strike the ball and, of course, it does matter, both to your score on the course and also to your confidence on the practise range. When striving for new habits there will, inevitably, be a period of uncertainty with your new technique. Whether implementing a grip change, a small change in your stance, or a substantial swing change, it will take time for the changes to become comfortable. In the interim, your results may get even more unpredictable, making it even more difficult to commit to any changes you make.

The ball itself is the main problem. It is all too easy to get wrapped-up in thoughts of where the ball might end up. We often focus too hard on making contact with the ball instead of focusing on the swing we need to make the ball fly further and more regularly to the target. We've all heard the clichés ... 'let the ball get in the way of the swing' ... 'collect the ball with your swing' ... or, 'pretend the ball isn't even there'. However, it is almost impossible to completely ignore the ball and there is nothing to be gained by looking anywhere else, but we must ensure that, first and foremost, we swing THROUGH the ball and not AT the ball.

In all sports that involve a ball, we either hit or kick THROUGH the ball and don't stop AT the ball ... the follow through always being much longer than the backswing. I want you to think about your golf ball being struck in the same way ... i.e. on the way to your follow through. As a coach, I hate the word 'downswing' and I try to avoid using it if I possibly can. Why? ... because there isn't a great deal we can do about it. You should think about the club going backwards (away from the target) and forward (towards the target). The only reason the club goes upwards at all is due to the fact that we are bending forward in the set-up position so the swing is therefore naturally inclined. The club will automatically come back down again on the way forwards so we don't have to worry about that part of the swing.

These points are also covered during the 'Swing don't hit' chapter but, as the mental side of golf is so inextricably linked with the physical, what you are thinking is just as important as what you are doing. Mentally, we can all too easily associate mishits with swing faults. You will find yourself (or someone else) saying things like; 'you moved your head' or, 'you lifted your head' or some other misperceived and mythical physical fault. Chances are, you were hitting AT the ball hard instead of swinging smoothly THROUGH it. Chances are, you did not trust your swing. Chances are, you let the fear of the result inhibit your ability to commit to the swing you have been practising.

Trust and fear are two of the most important influences in the mental aspects of all sports or, indeed, in many facets of our normal lives ... making speeches, meeting new people, etc. Our performance can easily be influenced by the fear of the result ... or more accurately, the fear of failure. This fear leads to nervous tension, shaking hands and shaking knees: not the best things to be experiencing as you play your golf shot. But what are we afraid of? We are clearly not in fear for our lives when we play golf (except from errant golf shots from other players maybe!), but the symptoms can often be similar ... sweaty palms, shaking hands, racing heart, etc. Nerves, however, are inevitable in life, and in golf, and we all suffer them. Even the best players have nerves (imagine representing your continent in the Ryder Cup and being the first player to tee off), but they learn to play well despite their anxieties and are well trained in coping strategies that minimise the effects.

So, how do they cope? First of all, accept that being nervous is a natural human physical reaction ... you'd have to be practically asleep to avoid them entirely. With time, however, you will learn that you can play good golf even when you are nervous. You can still play good shots and hole important putts despite your nerves. Secondly, you need to build a solid routine for each type of shot you play ... full swing, pitch or putt. Your routine becomes the mental 'crutch' that you will begin to rely on and trust.

Building your routine takes practise. It doesn't just involve the physical motions you go through but also involves thinking in the same way each time. As you can imagine, it's the thinking part that is the most important ... you have to believe that the shot will be successful. It's far more common, however, to be distracted by thoughts of disaster. Your mind will see the potential pitfalls much more easily than it will see success ... if you let it!

9.2 Your Routine(s)

I say routines because the requirements of the short-game and putting are different from your power-swing. Putts and pitches are never the same from one shot, or day, to another ... they are always unique in some way. Your routine, for these 'feel' shots, may necessitate multiple practise swings (or putting strokes) to acquire just the right touch for the requirements of the shot. Conversely, your full swing routine can be stricter and more time-efficient; the shots being played from known distances and with the confidence that the club you have chosen will do the job with your usual swing. We have dealt with your putting routine and short-game routines in previous chapters, but the requirements for trust are at the core of routines.

As far as your full-swing routine is concerned, it should be about allowing the implementation of your dedicated practise when it matters most. The physical aspects of your routine will be different from player to player, but observe how better players go about the execution of the shot at hand. The mantra 'see it, feel it, do it' should always apply. The whole process should not take too long (somewhere between ten and fifteen seconds is ideal) ... anything too drawn out will only add to the tension. Your routine starts when it is your turn to play and you have your club in your hand. This evokes another important point. Once you have decided on the club for the shot, you must believe completely that it is the right club ... no doubts what-so-ever should enter your head. If, subsequently, your choice proves to be wrong we 'live and learn' from the mistake, but we should never have doubt in the club at any point during the routine.

Okay, you are ready to go. You have 'seen' the shot you want to play, you are confident in the club you have chosen and you have made yourself aware of the hazards involved ... you will not, however, allow yourself to be distracted by these hazards whilst playing the shot ... you must focus only on your target. Your target should not be vague or unspecified (such as; the middle of the fairway or just the green), your target should be small and specific (such as; a single tree trunk in the distance or the edge of a bunker or the flagstick itself). If you subsequently miss your small target you should still be in reasonable position, but if you miss a loosely specified target you could end up anywhere.

Your routine should be identical every time. Down to the exact second ... every time. There should be a definite point at which the final part of your routine begins. You might simply say 'ok', or 'let's go', or you might click your fingers. From this point on, your every move should be set in stone (learned from repetition during your practise sessions). You should move calmly and smoothly into position and 'pull the trigger' (i.e. start your backswing) at the same moment on every shot. This last part is crucial, as it is at the very last moment that erroneous thoughts and doubt can creep in to your mind and result in a hesitant and unconfident swing. If you miss your 'trigger-point' because you didn't commit, then you might as well start again.

What constitutes the ideal routine? ... you may ask. Here is my suggestion to start you off, but watch better players and get some ideas from them.

1. Visualise a successful shot. Stand directly behind the line of the shot and mentally 'see' the ball fly to your target. Imagine the shape and trajectory you want the ball to fly in. See only a successful result and don't be distracted by the hazards.

2. Feel the swing that will make the shot happen. You can make your practise swing from behind the ball, in-line with your target, or walk to the side of the ball and make a swing or two from there. Either way, the purpose of your practise swing is to feel your rhythm and the weight of the club in your hands. One or two swings (at the most) is sufficient, but if you usually have one swing before playing the shot then don't suddenly add a second as this is a break from your usual routine.

3. Execute without delay. This is the absolutely crucial part and should be completely set in stone. The way you make your final move into your set-up and place the club behind the ball is the ritual with which you must strike every blow. This ritual should be rehearsed again and again until you can do it without thinking about it. This should be the habit that you repeat automatically whilst executing every shot ... whether on the practise range or on the course.

Together with this physical routine (the physical movements you make) you must have a solid mental state of mind. You must think the same things every time you set up to the ball and strike the shot. Think only of success and do not hesitate over any part of the process. Any hesitation, or indecision, will result in an instantaneous attack of doubt ... a sure-fire killer of a successful golf swing.

In summary, you must *see* a successful shot, *feel* the swing that's going to make it happen and *trust* completely in that swing.

Your routine and belief should be equally comfortable whether you are playing a standard tee shot, your ball is halfway up a bank, or it's laying deep in the rough. These shots may require a little more improvisation of stance and posture but your pre-shot ritual and rhythm of swing should remain intact. The next chapter will help you deal with some of the awkward situations you might find yourself in.

CHAPTER 10

Awkward lies, hazards, weather and trees

10.1 We all get into trouble

An awkward lie describes any situation where your ball is not on the tee/fairway or is situated on anything other than flat land. Your ball may often be situated in long grass of varying depths and thicknesses. It may also be resting on a significant slope or lying in a bunker. Less commonly, your ball may end up in an old divot, an *animal scrape*, or you may have a restricted backswing. You will also, inevitably, be in the trees at some point. For the sake of your score, it is what you do next that will make or break that score for the hole being played or, indeed, your score for the rest of the round.

10.2 Rough

The most common awkward lie you will encounter is when your ball is off the fairway and settles in the rough. The rough, or longer grass flanking the fairway, can vary in depth from just a few inches to well over a foot or more. Your ball might be perched invitingly on top of the grass or it could be nestled near the bottom of the grass and obscured from view.

If you have been lucky, your ball may be 'teed-up' on top of the grass enabling you to play any kind of shot you wish. If you still have a significant distance to go, a fairway wood or hybrid/rescue club may be the best club to play ... you can simply sweep the ball off the top of the grass as you might when playing from the tee. If you're less lucky, your ball will be surrounded with grass by some degree or another.

Your ball may be 'sat-down' slightly, but a reasonable result is still possible

Your ball may be completely surrounded by grass

If you're lucky, your ball might even be 'teed-up' and any shot is possible

This is when good course management is needed. There may still be a long distance to the green and your instincts will be telling you that you need a long club to get there ... to make up for the distance you've lost. You may even think about your rescue' club, as that's what its name suggests ... it will rescue you from anywhere ... won't it?! Personally, I don't like the word 'rescue' to describe any golf club ... especially when it describes quite a long club that has very little loft. True, it is a more forgiving club than a long iron, as it has a much wider sole and will usually offer a better result from the fairway or tee, but, unfortunately, it may lead you to the conclusion that it will 'rescue' your ball from anywhere and any lie ... the reality, however, is that it won't!

If your ball is 'sat-down' in the rough, you need loft to get it out. You need to hit down on the ball a little more than usual and get to the bottom of the grass surrounding the ball. You need to trust that the loft of the club will get the ball up and you need to accept that the ball may not go very far. This concept is explored further in the course management chapter of this book ... the message being *take your medicine* ... meaning that, if you are already in trouble, don't make it worse!

If your ball is lying right down in the rough you need to get it back onto the fairway and take your chances from there. You will need to hit quite aggressively down on your ball, with a lofted club, in this situation. You need to trust that the loft on the club will get the job done and anything lower numbered (less lofted) than a seven-iron will struggle to get the ball out of a deep lie in the rough ... even then, a 9 iron or wedge will usually be a better option.

When playing a short approach shot from the rough around the green you will need to assess the lie very carefully. If the ball is 'down' in the grass it will be difficult to get it airborne quickly and your ball will not come out with much backspin ... and won't stop very quickly when it lands. Some recovery shots, therefore, may be out of the question. If your ball is on a bare lie, for example, you won't be able to slide the club under it very easily and the ball will probably fly quite low ... a soft-landing shot to a flag location that is close to you is probably unrealistic. So, 'take your medicine' and play a modest recovery which, may not leave you near the flag but won't get you into even more trouble either. Sometimes the best you can do is leave your ball fifteen to twenty feet from the hole and still be pleased with this result.

You may, however, have a good lie in the rough and feel you can play a normal short pitch onto the green. Your ball may fly slightly higher than if playing from fairway grass (as there is more room under the ball) but you still need to allow for the extra resistance of the longer, thicker grass and your swing will require a little more power to accelerate through it. Make a few practise swings through a similar looking piece of grass nearby (be careful not to dislodge your ball from its resting place by practise swinging too close to it) and feel the resistance as your club passes through it; this will help you to gauge the amount of power the shot requires. Also, be aware that, due to the possibility of grass being trapped between the clubface and the ball at impact, your ball will usually fly out with less backspin than from a fairway lie ... therefore, allow for this in the assessment of your shots from the rough around the green.

10.3 Slopes

Unfortunately, very few golf courses are flat and even the flattish ones will still have banks and slopes that you will encounter. The first imperative, when your ball is on an inclined lie, is ... don't fight the slope or play into it! Golf aside, our tendency, when standing on a slope, is to keep ourselves vertical with the world by leaning into the slope, thus, keeping ourselves in our familiar upright human position. However, this doesn't work in the golfing world as you will end up swinging down into an upslope or upwards on a down-slope. On side-slopes your normal set-up position and posture may even lead you to miss the ball altogether. The additional 'cardinal sin' for all sloping lies is to lose your balance, but this is what any slope will tend to encourage. You must, therefore, swing within your usual power limits and it is advisable to take a longer club than usual and swing with a smooth 'quiet' rhythm.

There are four basic sloping lies that you might encounter on the golf course. Playing downhill or uphill, or with the ball below or above your feet. Let's deal with each one separately.

10.3.1 Ball above your feet

This is the easiest situation to adapt to but you still need to change your set-up and the feel of your swing. The simplest way to improvise for this situation is to hold the club further down the grip than usual; this will orientate the ball nearer to its natural position in relation to you. Stand a little more upright than you usually do and with your weight bias slightly towards

your toes as the slope will tend to throw you back as you swing. Your swing will feel a little more rounded (more around your body than usual) and you should allow for the possibility of the ball hooking, drawing or pulling, due to the more rounded (flatter) swing ... so aim accordingly. Restrict your swing slightly, especially in the backswing, and allow the longer club you've chosen to do

The set-up position when the ball is above your feet.

its job (as suggested in the introduction to slopes 10.3).

10.3.2 Ball below your feet

Sometimes called a *'hanging lie',* this is probably the most difficult slope situation you will experience. In simple terms, you should remember what to do as everything is the opposite of 'ball above your feet' as described above. With the ball below your feet the most likely danger is *topping,* or *slicing.* We need to bend slightly further forward than usual but keep you weight bias more towards your heels ... once again, be aware that gravity will tend to pull you off balance and down the slope ... particularly on this one. Take a longer club than you feel you need from the distance you have to the green and hold as high as possible on that club. Due to the fact that you are bending forwards more than usual, your swing will go up and

down at a steeper angle. Therefore, if you tend to slice the ball, this lie is likely to magnify the curvature of the ball ... so, once again, aim accordingly. As before, restrict your backswing a little and swing smoothly ... well within your usual effort. You must always strive to swing THROUGH the ball but don't come all the way up to your usual finish ... the phrase

Bend further forwards with your weight biased towards your heels a little more than usual

'down and through' should be your mantra here.

10.3.3 Playing steeply uphill

The obvious reality here is that your ball will not fly as far as it would on the flat. The uphill slope will 'kill' the last part of the ball's flight and certainly won't allow much roll upon landing. The natural temptation is to lean into the slope but this will make your downswing much too steep and you will, more than likely, bury the club into the ground without any follow through. With an uphill slope (and the

The set-up position for an uphill lie

same for downhill) you should feel that you level your shoulders with the slope. Therefore, on an uphill slope you will have slightly more weight on your back foot and also feel that your shoulders tilt backwards down the hill. Play the ball a little further forward in your stance than usual. As with all the other slopes, you must restrict your swing power and expect the ball to fly much higher than usual and stop very quickly upon landing ... a much longer club is usually required. You won't be able to reach your usual follow through position as the slope will tend to throw you backwards, but you must still get through the ball as much as possible. For this reason, you may tend to *pull* the ball from this lie so be aware of this as you aim.

10.3.4 Playing steeply downhill

Once again, reverse the advice above and you won't go far wrong ... with the exception that the ball with

You must level your shoulders with an uphill or downhill slope

travel even further than you might expect. The ball will fly at a lower trajectory and will roll significantly more when it lands. Therefore, if you have to fly your ball over a hazard, or other obstacle, perhaps think again. I don't suggest, however, that you take a shorter club than you usually would from that distance as, with all sloping lies, you should swing well within the limit of your usual power-swing in

153

order to maintain your balance. Position the ball a little further back in your stance than you usually would for the club you have selected. As per the advice for uphill slopes, level your shoulders with the lie-of-the-land and set a little more weight on your front leg. Keep your backswing shorter than usual and swing with a smooth rhythm ... ensure you don't rise up to your full finish position or you will be likely to *thin*, or *top,* the ball. You should feel that you 'chase the slope' with your follow through ... accentuating a low downward angle through the strike with the ball. Be prepared for a low-flying trajectory and a ball-flight which will tend to push, fade, or slice off-line ... neither will your ball stop quickly upon landing.

10.3.5 In summary of sloping lies

Of course, there may be occasions when two of the four slopes merge and conspire to offer a new challenge. However, with a sound knowledge of how to deal with the four basic inclines you will soon learn to improvise for any combination of slope you may experience. Whatever kind of slope your ball is lying on, you must keep your balance, swing within yourself, and change your set-up accordingly. Make a cautious shot selection and don't be too ambitious with your recovery ... especially from downhill slopes and hanging lies.

10.4 Water Hazards

What is a *hazard*? A hazard is a golfing term used to describe specific obstacles designed to 'trap' your ball if you hit an errant shot. Water hazards take the form of lakes, ponds, streams and ditches. These are either marked with red or yellow stakes depending on their location across, or alongside, the hole you are playing. Different rules apply in each situation and you should refer to the rules of golf booklet available freely to all golfers. These obstacles are usually full of water but occasionally they are dry, meaning you may find your ball and decide that it is playable. However, the rule of golf that you must remember is that you are not allowed to 'ground' your club in a hazard; doing so will incur a two-shot penalty (or loss of hole in match-play). You can 'legally' play the shot but you must be careful not to touch the ground (or water) behind the ball as you set up to the ball. Also, be careful with any practise swings you make as you must not disturb anything growing around your ball; otherwise the same penalty will be incurred. By all means, consider playing the shot if you feel it is within your capabilities (you can even play the ball out of very shallow water), but it may often be more prudent to 'take your medicine' and drop out of the hazard with just the one penalty stroke added.

10.5 Bunkers

Also known as sand traps (or simply, *traps*), bunkers are also officially *hazards*, though they are not defined by coloured stakes. Thus, the same rule applies and you must not 'ground' your club, or touch the sand with your club, prior to executing the shot. A penalty of two strokes applies if you touch the sand behind the ball with your club during your set-up, or even on your backswing, so be wary.

Bunkers fall into two main categories … fairway bunkers and greenside bunkers. Fairway bunkers are cunningly placed to *trap* your tee shots or second shots on long holes and greenside bunkers are positioned to punish a misdirected approach to the green. Fairway bunkers tend to be large and relatively shallow and, with only a few minor adjustments to your set-up, a relatively normal shot can be played. However, some fairway bunkers (especially on links courses) can be much deeper and, very often, all you can hope to do is get your ball out of the bunker and back into play. You should attempt to escape from these bunkers in the same way you would for a greenside bunker (by using a *sand wedge*) and accept that you cannot gain much ground.

10.5.1 Playing from a shallow fairway bunker

Your only real hindrances here are that the ball will be slightly embedded in the sand and that your stance will be less stable than normal (remember how it feels trying to run on the beach). A clean strike is, therefore, more difficult to achieve and you are quite likely to lose your footing if you swing too hard. There are a few things you can do, however, to make a successful shot more likely.

Firstly; as the sand is likely to shift slightly under your feet when you swing, you should swing a little easier than normal and, therefore, take a longer club than you would usually use from that distance (be aware, however, of the bunker's 'lip' in front of you as you need sufficient *loft* to clear it). Secondly; the rules allow us to embed our feet into the sand in the process of taking our usual set-up position and you can use this advantage to gain a firmer footing (you may have wondered why the top players you see on TV, wiggle their feet into their stance when playing from sand?). This action has the added benefit of being able to feel the depth and texture of the sand you are playing from and, consequently, overcomes the rule that does not allow us to 'test the surface' of the sand with our club prior to the shot ... but we are allowed to do it with our feet. Thirdly; you should play the ball slightly further back in your stance than usual for the club you have chosen. This will help to ensure that we strike the ball before the sand; any *'fat'* connection with the ball will produce a significant loss of distance. Again, don't forget the rule that doesn't allow you to 'ground' your club, or touch the sand, on your backswing ... a two-stroke penalty being the punishment.

In summary, take more club (be sure you can clear the bunker lip of the bunker), swing easy and play the ball further back in your stance. Also, be aware, that if you strike the shot cleanly the sand will impart more backspin than usual ... this is another reason to take a little more club from a fairway bunker than you normally would. If you play on a course with deep pot-bunkers in the fairway then, mostly, your only option is to escape and accept that you won't gain much distance (you may even have to go sideways or backwards on some occasions ... hard medicine to swallow!). Refer to the techniques described for greenside bunker shots below.

10.5.2 Greenside Bunker Shots

Greenside bunkers are far more prevalent on most courses than fairway bunkers and, the chances are, you will end up in one reasonably regularly. Learning to escape (preferably first time) is therefore crucial to your lowest score and will help remove those disaster-holes from your round. Bunkers, and the flag positions near to them, are placed cunningly to trap your approach shot to the green ... the hole often being cut just the other side of a bunker tempting you into a risky shot. Therefore, the most obvious ploy that will help your bunker play is to be wary of the 'trap' that is set and avoid them in the first place. If you are a higher handicap player or relative beginner, you should aim away from the bunkers and accept that a long putt is much more preferable than a bungled bunker escape. If you are a more experienced player you might still aim away from the bunker guarding the flag, but look to 'feed' your ball nearer to the flag with clever use of the wind or the contours of the green.

There are several levels of greenside bunker play ranging from entry level to expert. If you a beginner, or inexperienced player, getting your ball out of the bunker first time and anywhere on the green is your primary concern. As your technique and confidence improve, getting the ball out of the bunker will become more assured. You will, ultimately, begin to think about getting your ball near enough to the hole to sink your first putt.

At entry level, anywhere out of the bunker is better than being stuck in it ... although rocketing off into another bunker on the other side of the green isn't much better either! The first thing to understand, about the typical green-side recovery shot, is that we are NOT attempting to hit the ball at all. This is a difficult concept for new players to understand and involves a completely different feel from the good strike we strive for from the tee or fairway. Why don't we simply pitch the ball out of the bunker as we might for any other short shot from around the green? The reason is that the ball will be slightly embedded into the sand which makes a normal contact (i.e. ball then ground) extremely unlikely ... golfers have, therefore, come up with a better way. Through evolution of technique and equipment we have learned to use the sand to our advantage and 'blast', 'explode', or 'splash' the ball out of the bunker together with the sand it is resting on ... hence the commonly used phrases 'explosion shot' and 'splash shot'.

One of the foremost prerequisites for a successful greenside bunker shot is loft (height), either to get the ball up over a high lip in front of you, or to stop it relatively quickly when it lands. The easiest way to achieve this loft is to use your most lofted club, namely; your sand wedge (or possibly your lob wedge if you have one). At beginner or intermediate level, you should usually consider your sand-wedge to do this job as it is specially designed for this purpose. The sole of the club is manufactured to allow the club-head to slide through the sand without digging into it and allow the ball to fly out with the sand. Essentially, the ball flies out of the bunker on a 'bed' of sand and the sand-wedge helps us to achieve this result more easily.

10.5.2.1 Beginner level explosion shot

As we are attempting to use the sand and not, directly, hit the ball, the sand will absorb a significant amount

of the club's speed as it enters. We, therefore, need a relatively powerful swing … much more powerful than you might imagine from close to the green. The swing we need is, consequently, much more akin to your power-swing than your pitching swing. The small

Your club should enter the sand with sufficient power to 'blast' the ball out

exception being, that we need to keep the clubface '*open*' through the striking zone, rather than let it close over as we naturally would in the power-swing. This is important in order to maintain the *loft* of the club and hence send the ball

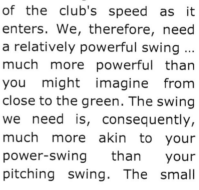

The feeling of sliding the club underneath the ball is a good one

sufficiently upwards out of the bunker. In very simple terms, we are trying to slide the club-head underneath the ball with sufficient power for the club to drive through the sand ... taking the ball with it. Keeping the clubface *open* through the sand is also vital to getting the ball up and out, otherwise you will simply smother the ball in sand and will be very lucky to get the ball out at all.

There are two major things that can go wrong with your bunker shot. One; we leave the ball in the bunker, or two; we hit the ball too cleanly by accident and it rockets off into trouble the other side of the green. To avoid either of these potential disasters, we need to ensure that two basic principles are followed. Firstly, we must swing with sufficient power to get the club through the sand and, secondly, we must hit the sand and not the ball. Some instruction will advise you to hit an inch or two behind the ball, which is fine, but I prefer to think of sliding the club under the ball as you are less likely to dig into the sand in this way. My thinking being that, it's just as difficult to strike the sand at an exact point behind the ball, as it is to strike the ball cleanly in the first place.

This is the thinking behind the shot, but the set-up to the ball is equally as important as the swing itself. We need to drive the club down and under the ball so, set up to the shot with the ball slightly forward of the middle of your stance and set a little more weight on your front foot. This 'leaning' ahead of your ball will make your swing a little steeper than usual and ensure you get the club into the sand ... down and through ... down and through ... should always be your mantra here. Take a wide stance with your knees bent a little more than usual as we need to swing slightly lower than the ball. You should feel, therefore, that this 'lower' set-up will help you slide the club under the ball. *Open* the clubface slightly (i.e. turn the toe of the club away from you), but *open your stance* a little *as* well to offset this (see glossary).

Once in position, make a long, smooth and relatively powerful swing with a generous follow through. However, do not rise up to your normal

trophy finish but hold your knees slightly bent through, and beyond, contact with the sand. You must not try to scoop the ball up, or lift the ball out, with any conscious swing action ... simply swinging down, under and through with power and commitment (whilst keeping the clubface open) will allow the ball to rise up and out from the sand.

The set-up position for a standard green-side bunker shot

This fully committed technique will make it much more likely that your ball will come out of the bunker first time; we must, however, ensure that we don't succumb to the second problem of the ball travelling way too far using this close-range powerful swing. The danger lies in hitting the ball too cleanly (i.e. hitting the ball before the sand) or hitting the ball halfway up. This clean (*thin*) contact, combined with the power of swing we are suggesting, will no doubt send your ball way off into the distance into even more trouble. To avoid this outcome, we need to be aware of a few things in the set-up and follow through.

As the rules of golf don't allow us to ground our club behind the ball prior to playing the shot, we need to hover the club above the ground (or, in this case, the sand) before we swing. This is not an easy concept to grasp initially, but with practise it will become more comfortable. Despite this added distraction, we are attempting to swing the club underneath the ball and therefore lower than usual. To make this easier, we need to lower our 'centre of gravity' or to give it a more technical term ... *'swing centre'* (the centre of you, that the club swings around ... considered to be the top of your sternum). This is made possible by widening your stance, twisting your feet lower into the sand, and also by bending your knees more than usual. The crucial thing for your swing is that you don't come up out of this position too early in your follow through. Therefore, don't attempt to come up to your full trophy finish position as you are likely to come up and out of the shot too soon and probably thin or top the ball. Hold your knees bent through impact and accept a slightly curtailed follow through position. However, you must ensure that your club is accelerating through the impact zone or you won't move the ball very far.

10.5.2.2 Intermediate/Expert Level

You will not need to add hugely to your technique, or your thinking, from that outlined above. However, at this level, we are hoping to get the ball somewhere near the pin and not just out of the bunker and somewhere on the green. To achieve this, you will need to learn the feel for taking more, or less, sand in order to control the distance the ball flies and also understand that backspin is imparted by the sand onto the ball. The general rule is, that more sand will create a lower ball flight and more roll (ideal for lower lipped bunkers and longer bunker shots) and less sand, taken from under the ball, will pop the ball up higher with more backspin and therefore stop much more quickly (ideal for 'pot bunkers' and/or shorter shots with little room between the edge of the bunker and the hole). By varying the amount of sand you take with the ball as you swing through, you can learn to control the distance and trajectory of your bunker shots according to the situation you are in.

Of course, greenside bunkers are rarely completely flat. You will have to contend with the down-slopes, side-slopes and up-slopes that any 'bowl-shaped' hole in the ground will present. Follow the general rules for slopes (chapter 10.3) but be careful to maintain the angle of attack down, into and through the sand: this angle of attack must be preserved, regardless of the slope you are standing on. You will need to vary the ball-position in relation to your feet (i.e. nearer to or further away from the target within your stance) in order to keep this angle of attack consistent. You will also need to adjust the level of your shoulders and weight distribution within your stance so that you are swinging with the slope and not fighting it.

10.5.3 Bunker Shot Summary

Once you have acquired the basic technique and understood the fundamental philosophy behind bunker play, you must practise regularly to refine your feel for the different shots and situations you will encounter around the course. If you are an aspiring player, being able to get 'up and down' in two shots from a greenside bunker will not only reduce your scores, but also reduce the pressure you may otherwise feel on your approach shots if your bunker play is suspect. With good bunker play, you can keep a good round going despite hitting some dubious approach shots. If you are a beginner, or high handicapper, being able to escape from a bunker first time and allow the opportunity for no more than two putts, could radically improve your rounds.

Follow these techniques and, quite soon, you will be walking into any bunker with a new-found confidence in your ability to recover.

10.6 Playing in the wind

Wherever you play your golf, the wind makes the game a lot more difficult. However, with experience and understanding of the principals involved, you can learn to be less affected by a breezy day. If your course is by the sea, or on top of a hill, then this chapter is especially important to your score.

The wind will not only affect your ball, but also your balance and your concentration. The wind howling around your ears and flapping at your trousers when you putt can be equally as disruptive as it can be to your ball-flight from the tee. You can't ignore the wind but you can learn to use it to your advantage, and, most importantly, learn not to fight it.

The first rule of thumb is to keep the ball low to the ground. Once your ball gets up high into the air it is at the mercy of every gust of wind. It be buffeted offline and the distance it travels severely impaired. Even if you are playing downwind (wind directly behind), your ball can be 'knocked down' out of the air and not fly as far as you might have executed (although the ball will still go further than usual as it won't stop very quickly when it lands). YOU will also be affected by the wind. Your balance and concentration will be affected greatly and it is all too easy to lose your cool and give up too soon. However, remember that the wind will affect everyone playing that day, and the scores are likely to be much higher than on a calm day ... so, stay patient and make the best of every shot you play.

Whichever direction the wind is coming from there are some basic concepts that we should bear in mind. Your balance will be affected ... so widen your stance. Your swing will be affected ... so shorten it slightly. Your mind will be affected and you are likely to become irritated ... so stay calm. Sometimes, a *bogey* is a really good score on a difficult hole on a windy day, so you won't have lost anything to 'the field'. In *match-play,* you may even win the hole with a bogey or worse!

There are, essentially, three wind directions to be concerned with ... into the wind, downwind, and across the wind (with almost infinite combinations thereof). First, and foremost, you must know where the wind is coming from ... but how can you tell for sure? You might simply look at the flag, or throw some grass in the air to see which way it blows. However, the wind at ground level can be confusing. The flag (and/or the grass) may both blow in the same direction, but the wind higher up (where your ball is going to be) may be completely different. The wind at ground level is affected by trees and other significant objects such as; banks, sand dunes and even buildings close by. There are other ways, however, of determining where the wind is coming from.

1. Be constantly aware of the wind direction. You will probably be mindful of the wind direction when you start your round as there is often a large flagpole near the clubhouse, or a practice area with multiple flagsticks, to indicate this. This knowledge may help you as you go around the course, as long as you can orientate yourself with each hole as you play. For instance, if the first hole is playing into the wind and the second hole runs in the opposite direction, you know already know where the wind is before you play the second hole. This gets harder as you go around the course with each twist and turn you make (especially if you don't know the course very well). Also, be aware that the wind direction can change throughout the course of a four-hour round ... especially on seaside courses as the wind changes with the tide.

2. Flags on other greens. The teeing-ground of the hole you are currently playing maybe sheltered from the wind. Likewise, the

flagstick you are playing towards may be protected by trees or mounds surrounding it and may not seem affected at all by the wind. So, be observant as you walk around the course and check the flags of adjacent holes as you pass by (especially ones in more open locations). Constantly keeping abreast of the wind direction can save much confusion.

3. The clouds. Assuming there are some on the day you play, keep looking up at them before you decide where the wind is coming from. The clouds are unaffected by anything at ground level and will always give a true picture of the predominant wind direction. The wind direction of the clouds may contradict other information you are observing ... but go with the clouds if you are in any doubt.

4. Watch your fellow players. Of course, on some days the wind is gusting, unpredictable and hard to know for sure where it is coming from. One final clue, however, is to watch the ball flight of your opponent's shot. You may not know the exact club they have used but, when all else fails, it may just give you a modicum of insight into wind strength and direction.

10.6.1 Playing into the wind

This is generally the most disruptive wind direction. Not only will it cause the hole, or shot, to play longer, this wind direction will increase the effects of any side-spin you create ... making it more difficult to control direction (especially if you slice … one of the most common problems). Your instinct, when playing into the wind, may entice you to hit at the ball harder than you would normally; especially with your driver off the tee. However, the harder you hit AT the ball the more backspin you will impart; this will cause the ball to *'balloon up'* and stall in the wind. Subsequently, this higher than normal ball-flight will exaggerate the loss of distance further still.

The secret, however, is to take a much longer club than usual, from any given distance, and actually swing more softly … we call this a *knockdown shot*. This shot will allow the ball to fly lower than usual and with reduced backspin, therefore, providing a more penetrating ball-flight. The *knock-down* shot is useful for all wind directions (and escaping from underneath trees!), so, here's how to play it.

10.6.2 The Knockdown Shot

The set-up position for the knockdown shot

The main objective with this shot is to keep the ball lower than it would normally fly with the club you have chosen. When playing into the wind, this club should be one, or two, or three, or sometimes even more clubs longer than you would use from that distance on a calm day. A longer, lower lofted club will hit the ball lower …

but not if you swing harder as this will increase backspin and make the ball climb higher into the wind.

There are three key factors involved in playing this shot. One; play the ball further back in your stance, allowing your hands to hang naturally and slightly forward (i.e. towards the target) of the ball than usual: the shaft angle will also lean forward toward the target. By setting up in this position, your chosen club will have even less *loft* than usual and, therefore, will ensure that the ball flies lower (provided that this position is maintained through impact). This is the second key to a successful *knockdown* shot. This

The set-up angles must be maintained through impact and beyond

hands-ahead-position at set-up must be maintained through impact and into the follow through. If your club-head overtakes your hands too soon, the loft that you are so desperately trying to reduce will be added back on again at impact and your ball will fly too high. Finally, ensure that you swing very much within your normal full-power effort. Feel that you don't swing back quite as much as usual and that your follow through is also slightly restricted. This shot requires a developed *feel* through practise and a reasonable skill level to begin with. If you don't believe you have the necessary skill just yet, make sure that, at the very least, you take a much longer club than usual and swing it a little easier than normal.

10.6.3 Playing with the wind

When playing downwind the situation is much easier. Being able to reach your target is not so much of an issue and any side-spin, imparted accidentally, is also negated somewhat ... however, there are still pitfalls to be aware of. The main one being that your ball is unlikely to stop quickly when it lands ... which is further magnified when the ground is firm. Your ball will, of course, fly a little further through the air with the wind behind and you can afford to play a slightly shorter, more lofted, club, but unless the greens are very soft your ball will take a big first bounce. Therefore, be wary, if you are attempting to carry your ball over a hazard, as you may get into more trouble behind the green if your ball won't stop.

10.6.4 Cross-winds

A well-struck shot will barely be affected by a light to moderate wind, but a shot that slices or hooks in the same direction as the wind is blowing can be exaggerated by any strength of wind. A strong wind, however, will affect all golf shots and you will need to allow for its effects. If your ball naturally curves in the opposite direction to the wind direction then your ball flight may not be affected very much. If your natural ball flight curves the way the wind IS blowing, however, you need to be careful, as sometimes you cannot aim far enough 'off-target' (due to trees, for example) to allow the ball to curve back. It would be useful, therefore, to learn how to *fade or draw* the ball into the prevailing wind direction for these circumstances (especially if you regularly play on windy courses). We call this 'holding the ball up against the wind'. If you are right-handed and the wind direction is left to right, a draw shaped shot (in this case, right to left) will 'hold' the ball straighter in the wind. If you are left-handed with the same wind direction then you would require a fade shot and vice versa.

10.6.5 Putting in the wind

A brief word about putting in the wind as you may not be aware of how much a substantial wind can affect this part of your game. The wind will, at a minimum, test your patience and concentration with its constant noise in your ears and fluttering of your clothing. It will also affect your balance so you will need to improvise your usual set-up to incorporate a wider, more stable, stance.

A strong wind will also affect your ball as it rolls ... especially on fast greens. Uphill and downhill putts will be affected the most, but if the wind is blowing in the same direction as the *break* on your putt your ball will curve even more than usual. If you stoke your ball just a little too fiercely on downhill putts with the wind behind, you could easily putt straight off the green. Conversely, on uphill putts, you may need to strike the ball appreciably harder than you think (though you should guard against going too far past the hole as you don't want a four-foot, downhill, downwind putt for your next one.

10.7 Playing in wet weather

Rain, without any wind, won't have much effect on your ball-flight but it can have a dramatic effect on you, your equipment, and the condition of the course. If YOU get wet you will get cold very quickly and if your clubs get wet they become impossible to hold securely. The course will also be affected. Puddles may suddenly appear in line with your shot and your ball will stop more quickly on landing; the greens will also become much slower to putt on.

Course conditions can be overcome, but how YOU react is far more important. You may feel suddenly disillusioned if it starts raining halfway round, or you may not be keen to go out if it's raining before you start. If you are prepared, however, both mentally and practically, you can have a big advantage over the rest of field who will, undoubtedly, be in the wrong frame of mind either before, or during, the round. You could well, therefore, be competing against only half the field, at best.

There are ways you can cope more easily with the wet. A good quality waterproof suit will, at least, keep you and your clothes dry ... although make sure it is designed for golf as hiking-type outdoor-wear does not offer sufficient flexibility for you to swing your golf club freely. Keeping your clubs dry is a much harder task. Unless you have a very expensive waterproof bag, an endless supply of dry towels and a caddy, it's almost impossible. Assuming you don't have the luxury of all or any of the above, then the simplest way is not to bother at all ... let your clubs get soaking wet and use a good pair of specially designed wet-weather gloves. It is never ideal to play in a pair of gloves (rather than your usual one glove), but the wetter everything gets, the better these gloves work ... being able to hold your clubs securely far outweighs the minor detail of an extra glove. So, before you play, ensure you have seen a detailed weather forecast and go out prepared for anything that the weather can throw at you.

10.8 When it's cold

Playing golf in winter can still be a very enjoyable experience and, unless you live in a sub-tropical climate, is something you need to prepare for, or not play at all for months which is not good for your golf!

The first prerequisite is, of course, to keep yourself warm, and the secret to this (as for any outdoor winter pursuit), is 'layering'. You may start off cold but you will warm up surprisingly quickly and need to be able to remove a couple of layers or so as you progress into your round.

A thin thermal base layer is your starting point ... at least for your body ... and maybe your legs as well on really cold days. Over this, wear your golf shirt as you may get down to this layer once you warm up. The next layer should be a wool sweater or lightweight fleece and your final layer should be a wind-proof or water-proof layer as a first barrier to the elements.

The last and most important parts of you to keep warm are your hands. It is very difficult to play good golf with freezing cold hands, but the problem is magnified as we don't really want to play golf in thick woolly gloves either! For sure, there are specialist thermal golf gloves available to buy, but these are much thicker than is convenient in order to achieve our normal grip. By far the most effective way, in my opinion, is to use your normal single glove (if you usually wear one) to play your shots with, but use thermal waterproof mittens with heat pads inside as you walk between shots. You can get disposable heat-pads from most golf shops or hiking shops and mittens are sold by most golf brands and made specifically for golf. However, make sure they are a big enough size to accommodate the heat pads and also allow them to be slipped off easily between shots.

Finally, be aware that golf balls do not perform at their best in very cold conditions and allow for this in your club selection. Ironically, your ball may not fly quite as far, but it won't stop as quickly either if the ground is still partially frozen from the cold!

10.9 Awkward lies summary

This chapter will, hopefully, help you deal with most of the hazardous and unusual situations you will encounter during many, if not all, rounds of golf. With practise, you will be able to adjust your set-up and swing for sloping lies, escape from underneath trees, control your ball in the wind and cope with anything the weather can throw at you. Combine your new-found 'escapology' skills with good decision-making (described in the following chapter) and you will quickly learn to think and play like the better player you aspire to be.

CHAPTER 11

Take Your Medicine (Course Management)

11.1 What do we mean?

The phrase 'take your medicine' is a commonly used term in golf, meaning that, with a sensible approach, you can recover from difficult situations around the golf course without completely wrecking your day. The temptation to make up for a poor shot by attempting a beyond-heroic recovery shot is very strong within us all. You may have topped your tee shot, landed in the trees or missed a short putt on the previous hole, but we need to accept these challenges as part of the game ... and not attempt a miracle recovery or make a rash choice of shot because we are angry. Sometimes 'taking your medicine' might mean playing sideways, or even backwards to get your ball back into play. This is a tough decision to take as it is a challenge to accept that we cannot gain any distance with the next shot. With experience (usually a 'painful' one!), you will learn that attempting shots beyond your capability, or making bad choices in frustration, can turn an ugly situation into something much worse.

11.2 Improve from the hole backwards

By improving all areas of your golf game, you will learn that one bad shot doesn't necessarily mean you can't make a reasonable score on that hole or win that hole in match-play. In match-play, staying patient and making the possible best score will keep the pressure on your opponent and force them to play a good hole to win it. In stroke-play, a six is a lot better than a ten, and that six will make a huge difference to your mental state compared with a one-hole disaster which may leave you wishing you were going home.

So, instead of concentrating solely on your driving (because you think it's most important), think about how improving your game from the hole backwards will help your strategy and state of mind. You may currently believe that you have to hit the green with every approach shot from the fairway because you don't have faith in your short pitching or bunker play. You may also believe that you have to pitch very close to the hole because you don't have faith in your putting. This kind of thinking is very common and leads to added pressure on every shot you play. However, by improving your putting, you reduce pressure on your pitching ... and by improving your pitching, pressure is taken off your approach play ... and by improving your approach play, with your short and medium irons, you will be more willing to accept a sensible recovery shot and yet still feel that you can make a reasonable score on the hole.

11.3 Use your handicap

You have a handicap for a reason ... it represents your current level of play. Of course, you want to improve it, but so many high handicappers play every hole as if they have a *'scratch'* handicap and can't resist 'having a go' at every narrow fairway or tight *pin* placement in the search of a par score. However, you probably aren't that scratch player just yet and learning to be patient is an acquired skill … one which scratch players and professional players alike need to practice in almost every round they play.

Keeping yourself 'in the game', so to speak, can do wonders for your confidence and keep you feeling positive after 'surviving' a potentially score-wrecking hole. It is often our lack of faith in our ability to recover from a bad shot, a bad hole, or a bad run of holes, that leads us to more disaster … but this is what your handicap is for. If you have a high handicap, you may become prematurely concerned during your round that your 'allowance' is running out, should you make a poor start. It becomes all too easy to begin attempting reckless recovery shots in a desperate bid to rescue your round. However, we must stay patient, as a run of solid holes, including a par or two or even a surprise birdie, can easily get you back on track. Experience will help you stay patient after your less than ideal start when previously you may have panicked, causing you to play beyond your means in an attempt to get your round back on track.

Therefore, try this little tip … add your handicap on at the start of every hole. For example, if you are an eighteen handicapper you get a one-shot allowance on every hole, so, by thinking in this way you can turn every par three into a par four, a par four into a par five and so on. If your handicap is 28 or 36 you get a two-shot allowance on most, or all of the holes … so, those long par fives are really par sevens! If you adopt this simple strategy it will stop you panicking when you realise you can't make a normal par. The truth is, that you may not need that many pars anyway to play to your handicap.

11.4 One shot at a time

This old cliché is more appropriate to golf than any other sport. No other sport is as truly 'one shot at a time' as golf is. Everything that happens on a golf course is completely controlled by YOU and nobody else ... therefore only YOU can 'mess it up'. It is easy to get ahead of yourself or let past errors play on your mind. We must, therefore, 'stay in the present' and focus only on the shot at hand and do the right thing for our score (even if that means going backwards). Always remember, that ... 'THE MOST IMPORTANT SHOT IN GOLF IS ALWAYS THE NEXT SHOT'.

11.5 Game-plan

Whatever your handicap, or however well you think you know your own course, you should always have a game plan. Your game plan is the strategy you have worked out beforehand, whilst in a calm frame of mind. This strategy should be relatively conservative in its ambitions ... this allows you to execute your strategy on the golf course with a calm confidence. Your plan should, of course, reflect your handicap, but even professionals don't play their driver off every tee, regardless of the length of the hole. Sometimes a longer second shot from the fairway is preferable to a shorter one from a bad lie in the rough. Thus, your game plan might suggest that you hit an iron from the tee on a long par four with a narrow fairway ... even if you can't reach the green in two. After all, that stroke-index number one hole is the hardest hole on the course for a good reason and a *bogey* is never a bad score on such a hole ... especially as virtually all golfers will receive, at the very least, a one-shot allowance on that hole.

11.6 Common strategy mistakes

We all make mistakes in judgement, but the key is to learn from them, and not keep making the same ones again and again. Ironically, most mistakes are made in the attempt to make up for previous mistakes. You may have just missed a short putt on the previous green and subsequently hit your next tee-shot in anger ... usually landing you in yet more trouble! You may have hit your ball into deep rough, or trees, and attempt an over-heroic escape to make amends for your error. There are myriad examples of compounding our errors, but here is my top ten of mistakes you should be wary of.

1. Hitting any shot in anger or frustration.
2. Attempting a recovery beyond your true capabilities.
3. Compounding your error with an over-ambitious next shot.

4. Hoping to carry your ball over a lake (or other hazard) which is right on the limit of your very best shot (i.e. not playing the percentages).
5. Choosing to hit your driver regardless of the strategy requirements of the hole.
6. 'Chasing' tight pin positions irrespective of the consequences.
7. Attempting to cut the corner of a *'dog-leg'* in order to shorten the hole.
8. Playing the high lob-shot to a close pin placement that induces a very low percentage of success.
9. Gambling on a perfect strike to negotiate whatever obstacle is in your way … therefore not allowing any margin for error.
10. Attempting, or experimenting with, any shot you haven't practised sufficiently before reaching the golf course.

11.7 Summary

Taking your medicine is paramount to your success. There are very few rounds of golf that we play during which we are not in some kind of trouble, even if it is only once or twice. What you decide to do when this happens can be 'make or break' to your success on the day. It can be equally challenging when we are playing well as it is when playing poorly. If we are progressing nicely during a round, but suddenly get into trouble, it can be even tougher to 'take your medicine' and accept a dropped shot or two … doing so can be one of the greatest mental challenges in the game.

CHAPTER 12

Effective Practice

12.1 Practise makes perfect. Right?

Well, not purely in itself it doesn't. As I have encouraged throughout this book, in order to improve, you must practise. What you practise and how you practise, however, are extremely important to the results you will experience. If you don't practise at all and just prefer to play frequently, that's understandable, but you should take the time (at least occasionally) to take stock and analyse each aspect of your game.

If you don't already do so, begin to break your game down into 'departments'. Analyse how many tee shots get you into trouble, how many approach shots miss the green and how many putts you average on each green. You may also take a closer look at how many shots you take after being in a bunker, or how many putts you take following a short pitch onto the green. Begin to analyse your 'departments' after every round in the following way.

1. Putts per green. Even though the professional tour statistics only count putts played from the putting surface itself, I believe we should count all our putts including those from just off the green ... this is a truer reflection of your putting skill ... or your chipping weakness! The nearer

your average is to two putts per green, or less, the better.

2. Up and downs. How many times did you get *'up and down'* (i.e. pitch and one-putt from within ten to forty yards of the green?). Beginners, or inexperienced players, will take an average of four, or even five shots from within this radius of the hole. If you can average less than three from this range then your scores will tumble down.

3. Greenside bunker escapes. A successful bunker escape happens the first time and results in a shot that remains on the green (rather than in more trouble the other side of the green). You should average less than three from a green-side bunker in order to achieve your goals.

4. Greens in regulation. This number describes the number of shots it should, ideally, take you to reach the green. If you are a *scratch player,* then hitting a green in 'regulation' requires that you hit a par three in one shot, a par four in two shots (or fewer) and a par five in three shots (or fewer). If you have any golf handicap higher than this, 'regulation' means adding one shot, or maybe two, to the scratch player's target. For example; an eighteen handicapper receives a one-shot allowance on every hole, so, even if you take one more shot (to reach the green) than described above, you can still make a (net) par ... assuming you can two-putt (further emphasising the importance of putting).

5. Fairways found from the tee. Excluding the par threes, there will be twelve to fourteen holes on the course that require an accurate and reasonably long drive from the tee. Your second shot, on any hole, is much more straightforward when played from the fairway or light rough alongside. Constantly playing out of long grass, trees, losing balls in hazards or regularly hitting out-of-bounds, is exhausting for your score ... and your mental stability. Record how many fairways you hit successfully from the twelve to fourteen holes that you hit your driver (or equivalent). If you wish, you could count shots that finish just off the fairway as long as they don't unduly penalise your next shot. Anything under sixty-percent success means that you are in trouble on virtually half, or more, of your tee-shots ... suggesting to you that you might need to do something about this part of your game.

From this kind of analysis, you can understand your strengths and weaknesses and begin to address the real issues within your game. For example; if you hit most of your fairways but average near to three putts per hole, then there's no necessity to practise with your driver very much. Practise the things you aren't as good at rather than the things you obviously relish ... we need to get better at the things we're not better at!

12.2 Technique v 'playing the game'

There are two, distinctly different, ways of practising your golf. You will, of course, need to acquire the correct techniques in order to improve your ball-striking, but you also need to replicate the pressure of playing *'one shot at a time'*, every four or five minutes, as we do when we play the game itself. It's not truly possible to replicate the intensity that you feel when playing on the course, but 'blasting away' with the same club for dozens of shots on the driving range isn't really playing the game of golf. There are times, however, when you are making improvements to your swing, putting stroke, or pitching technique, when hitting multiple shots with the same club, from the same spot, are necessary. Repetition is one of the keys to consistency and, therefore, ingraining or compounding a new swing feel with multiple swings is important. You must also practice playing ONE SHOT AT A TIME with different clubs, imagining you are playing the course for real, if you want to emulate the intensity you will feel on the course.

When in repetition-mode, it is more important to repeat your new swing feel with almost 'blind faith', without being too concerned where the ball goes (initially, at least). It will feel awkward and contrived to change anything in your current technique and there will need to be a period of 'forcing' the new action to happen … probably with indifferent results. Keep forcing and repeating the new action, however, and gradually the new feel will become more comfortable; you will begin to find some confidence in it. You will soon begin to hit a higher percentage of good shots with this new swing, but you must remember the exact feel of those good shots so you can do it again ... and again! In order to acquire new habits you need to give up the old ones, even if it means playing poorly for a while. This is your commitment to improvement and no-one gets to where they want to be without many ups and downs along the way!

Once you have practiced sufficiently in 'repetition mode', you need to put your new-found good habits to the test. Initially, however, this doesn't have to be on the course. In fact, playing golf is NOT practising! In just the same way, practising is NOT playing golf. We can, however, attempt to recreate the pressure we feel whilst playing one shot at a time on the course, by practising in this way for, at least, part of our driving range sessions. Use one club, for one shot at a time, resisting the temptation to hit another shot with the same club ... whatever the result. It will be even more tempting to 'have another go' if you completely mishit the first shot, but, as we do not get this opportunity in the game of golf for real, you need to fight this desire and get on with the next shot ... just as we have to accept the consequences of every shot we play on the course.

In this *game practising mode* you should play each shot with varying clubs and use your full 'on-course' routine for each one. Imagine a real shot you may have to play on a course you know well. It may be a tee shot on your least favourite hole or an approach shot over water that you fear. The more realistically you can imagine the fictitious scenario you face, the more 'pressure' you will add to the shot. After all, you are the only person who cares whether you succeed or fail, so, YOU are the only reason there is pressure at all!

Focus tightly on your target and imagine your ball flying to it. Make the practise swing that you feel will get the job done and commit to it fully when you strike the ball. If you are really disciplined, you will play an appropriate next shot from the imagined finishing position of your last shot ... as if you are playing the hole in real life.

You may not quite have the patience, or willpower, to do this but, at least, spend a reasonable amount of practise time hitting one shot, with one club and then changing to a different one ... preferably one that is very different from the last ... a driver to a wedge ... a hybrid to a six iron, for example.

12.3 In summary of effective practice

You may presume that any kind of practise is better than no practise at all, and to a degree this is true, but if you practise in a slightly more precise way then you will be much better prepared to play your best shots when it matters ... on the golf course. You will have already 'lived' some of the pressure you will face and also learned to deal with the reality of less than perfect results. Hitting balls can be great fun in itself and sometimes it's simply a good stress reliever or a good workout, but try to put some relevance into your practise sessions and you will be more able to take your 'range-game' to the course.

CHAPTER 13

Technical Stuff

13.1 The basics of ball flight and impact

Without getting overly complicated, it will help you to understand some of the technical aspects of the game in a little more detail. Understanding the terminology used to describe certain principles of the swing, and the factors affecting how the ball flies, will aid your development and, hopefully, stop you from 'guessing' in your attempts to fix certain problems. So, rather than 'clutching at straws' you can build sufficient knowledge to ensure you are practising the right things.

The first thing to understand, is that there are only five impact factors that affect the flight of the golf ball … yes, just five! Sometimes, it may feel that you can experience dozens of different results from what feels like the same swing, but it all comes down to these five things. These five properties, known as 'impact factors', combine to produce the nine most recognisable ball flights and variations thereof.

I will start by explaining these ball flights as it is a very rare golfer that uses the correct terminology to describe the shots they are producing. Without this understanding, this golfer will, subsequently, try to correct the wrong swing faults. The number of times I have heard a golfer say that they are hooking the ball when they are, in fact, pull-hooking the ball, I have lost count of. This may not seem an important misconception, but a *hook* and a *pull-hook,* are more than likely caused by two completely different swing characteristics ... the common result being that this golfer is trying to fix the wrong things. The following diagrams (for left and right-handers) will help you to understand the correct descriptions for our golf shots and offer an insight into the underlying issues that cause them to happen.

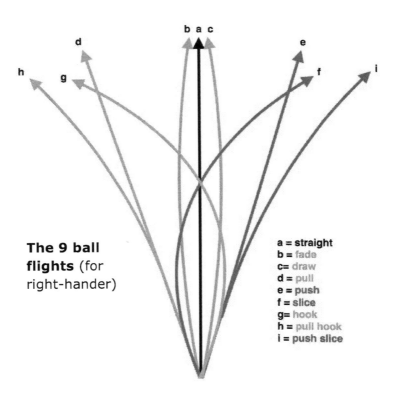

The 9 ball flights (for right-hander)

a = straight
b = fade
c= draw
d = pull
e = push
f = slice
g= hook
h = pull hook
i = push slice

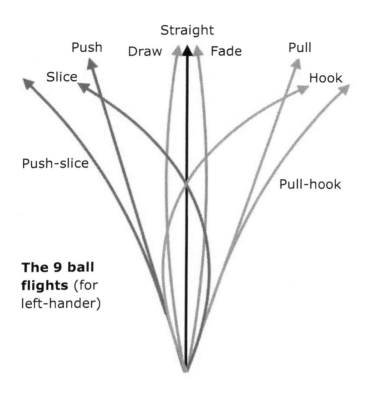

The 9 ball flights (for left-hander)

You will notice that only three out of the nine most common ball flights actually hit the target; a draw or fade being the favoured shot of professional players. Very few players hit the ball intentionally straight as the factors combining to produce this shot are not easily repeatable. Indeed, a straight shot WILL hit the target but many experts in the game will lightheartedly suggest that a straight shot only happens by accident.

Let us now explore the relationship between these ball-flights and the impact factors that cause them. The five impact factors, as alluded to earlier, are as follows:

1. Swing path: The direction in which the club-head is travelling as it passes through impact with the ball. Described as 'out-to-in', 'in-to-out', or 'in-to-in'.

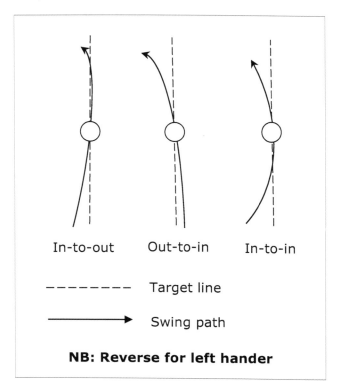

In-to-out   Out-to-in   In-to-in

‒ ‒ ‒ ‒ ‒ ‒ ‒   Target line

⟶   Swing path

NB: Reverse for left hander

2. Clubface angle: The angle of the clubface at impact - described as *square*, *open* or *closed*.

Closed clubface as seen from above

Open clubface as seen from above

Square clubface as seen from above

3. Angle of approach: The angle at which the club-head descends into impact with the ball. Can be described as too shallow or too steep, leading to poor consistency in ball-striking.

4. Centredness of strike: How near the *sweet spot* of the club-head the ball is struck from.

5. Club-head speed: How fast the club-head is travelling as it passes through impact with the ball.

These impact factors are present in every swing we make and the interrelationship between them is entirely responsible for the result of every shot. Some factors have more influence over certain aspects of the shot than others ... although they all affect the flight of your ball in one way or another. It would take another quite sizeable book to describe this relationship fully, but the following guide will help you understand what causes the most common missed shots. With a better understanding of what is going on with your golf club, you will have a much better chance of achieving the results you desire.

13.2 What Causes What?

There are far too many potential misses to include in such a short space, but the most common ones are described below. Any unsuccessful shot is either misdirected, mishit or a combination of the two.

Mishit shots are described as, *topped*, *thinned*, *fatted*, *shanked*, *toed*, etc. These non-centred strikes (factor no. 4 above) are mostly caused by poor timing (see 'swing don't hit' chapter) but are also influenced by the angle of approach (factor no. 3) being too steep or too shallow ... resulting in *'fat'* or *'topped'* shots.

Shanks (when the ball is struck from the *hosel* of the club-head), which shoot off at tangents, are caused by the club-head being *'outside'* the ball at impact and usually the result of the angle of approach being too steep ... the swing path (factor no. 1) is also likely to be excessively *out-to-in.*

Misdirected shots are generally described as; *slices, hooks, pulls, pushes, pull-hooks* and *push-slices.* These off-target shots are often struck reasonably 'sweetly' but, either start off in the wrong direction, or curve excessively offline during flight. These missed shots are predominantly caused, and affected, by the relationship between the swing path and the clubface angle through impact. There are, of course, dozens of potential combinations of exact club-head paths related to exact clubface angles, but the most common ones (as described below) cause the most commonly misdirected golf shots.

13.3 Slices, pulls and pull-hooks

This is where the most widespread misconceptions lie. You may be forgiven for wondering how your swing, which always feels the same to you, can produce shots that sometimes miss wildly to the left as well as to the right. A slice, for example, curves excessively in one direction whilst a pull-hook curves excessively in the opposite direction ... so how can this be possible?

The answer lies with the angle of the clubface at impact. Slices, pulls, and pull-hooks are predominantly caused by an out-to-in swing path ... one where the clubhead is generally outside *'the line'* or over and above the *'swing plane'* (commonly referred to as 'over the top'). When this happens, there is only one direction the club can be headed, and that is downwards too steeply and across your body excessively through impact. If the clubface happens to be at just the right angle of *'open'* at impact, then the ball will start off-target (to the left if you're right-handed and vice versa if you are left-handed) but curve gently back on target ... this SUCCESSFUL shot is called a fade. However, if the clubface is excessively *open* at impact then the ball will curve excessively away from the target and spin even more away from the target upon landing ... this unsuccessful shot is called a slice. With the same *over-the-top* swing path, if the clubface happens to be square or closed through impact, the ball will miss in the opposite direction ... causing either a *pull* or a *pull-hook*. If your swing is excessively *out-to-in* (over-the-top) you will probably slice your driver and longer clubs but *pull* your short irons (this is due to the club-head on a shorter iron being more likely to 'square-up' through impact than a longer club, such as a driver, where the clubface is more likely to remain open, causing a severe slice.

Almost all the players I see swing across themselves from *out-to-in through* impact so you are very likely to be doing the same. The cause is also usually the same ... hitting harshly down AT the ball instead of swinging THROUGH the ball to a well-balanced finish ... SWING, DON'T HIT. By following the principles described earlier in this book you should be able to eliminate (or at least reduce) the extent to which you *slice* or *pull*. Using the feelings of 'swish to the finish' and a more sweeping feeling through impact will help improve your swing path ... the clubface angle tends to evolve in response to this and will, therefore, help you to hit straighter more reliable shots.

13.4 The 'shank'

This badly mishit shot is sometimes described as the nearest thing to a perfect strike ... but it certainly

doesn't look or feel like one and it doesn't come from a particularly good swing either. Like most errant shots (in my opinion) this disastrous shot is caused by hitting too sharply downwards from the top of the swing. This leads to the club-head being thrown, or 'cast' out of position on its way down, ending up outside the target line ...

The position of the ball at impact, as seen from above

and, therefore, slightly the other side of your ball (NB: it's known as 'casting' as it's a little like casting a fishing rod ... but, in this case, it's being cast in the wrong direction ... namely; downwards/backwards).
The result is that the ball is struck from the extreme inside (heel-side) of the clubface and deflects off the inside angle of the hosel. The

The shank shot, as seen from the front

hosel used to be known as the 'shank' of the club, hence the unfortunate sounding name for this shot.

The shank-shot afflicts all players and actually tends to be a better player's problem with many a famous player suffering the dreaded shank at just the wrong moment in a tournament. 'The shanks' tend to come in batches of maybe three or four in a row and then mysteriously disappear ... it's no wonder that some players, superstitiously, cannot even say the word out loud!

In your early days of playing golf you may not be sure from which part of the club-head the ball has been struck, so seek professional advice if you experience the ball deflecting at tangents away from you. New players tend to hit the ball off the toe-edge of the club more frequently than the shank, so, you need to be sure which it is before you begin trying to fix it.

13.5 Swing-Plane ... a short explanation

Without getting too technical, your *swing-plane* is a combination of your *swing-path* and the angle at which your club descends into impact with the ball. Your swing plane can be described as, *on-plane,* or *over-the-plane,* or *under-the-plane*. Your ideal swing plane comes from a good set-up position (described in chapter 6.2) in which your club is automatically set at the ideal angle to swing at. The ideal golf swing-plane, however, is a curious mixture of around your body and up and down ... confusing to your brain as we are more used to our torso being completely upright when we make most physical dynamic motions.

There aren't many golf swings, performed by humans, at least, that follow exactly the same path in both the backswing and forward-swing ... even amongst the best of tour pros. On the whole, however, most great players bring the club downwards and forwards through the ball either, below the swing-plane (compared to the backswing), or on the same plane as the backswing (or sometimes very slightly above the plane). Most amateur players, however, bring the club down significantly 'over the top' of the

ideal approach into and through, impact. This 'over-the-top' downswing causes the majority of errant ball-flights (especially, slices, push-slices, pulls and pull-hooks ... the most devastating of misses).

Once your club-head (and it is only the club-head that we are concerned with here) gets outside of, or over the top of the swing-plane on its way down to the ball, it can only go one way through impact ... and that's from out-to-in. The descent is, therefore, steeper

Your ideal swing plane is set by a good set-up position. In a perfect world, the club will follow this 'plane' throughout the swing.

than ideal and it is this steep angle of approach from the outside that causes a dramatically curving and distance limiting ball-flight (and also shanks, pulls and pull-hooks).

13.6 Ball Position

As well as the swing itself, other factors can influence the path your club takes through impact and also the trajectory of the ball's flight. Where your ball is positioned in your stance is certainly one of them. Get this wrong and even the most perfectly executed swing will hit the ball off target. The term ball-position is generally referred to as the ball's location between your feet as viewed from directly in front of you; use a mirror to check the accuracy of your ball position ... all better players do. Of course, ball-position could also describe how close or how far away the ball is from you, but this is determined more by the length of the club you have selected.

The following diagram shows the appropriate ball position for each of the clubs in your bag. A newcomer to the game need not be concerned with precisely the right position for EVERY club but should ensure, at least, that the ball is located appropriately for each main section of the set – i.e. short clubs, medium clubs and long clubs.

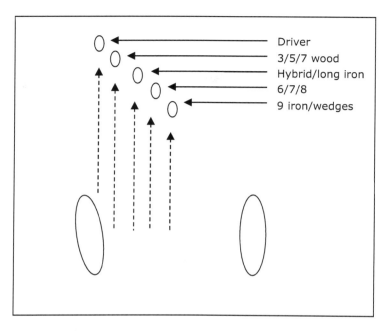

Ball positions for a right-handed player

Ball position is vital, as your clubs vary in length and, more importantly, *loft.* Your shorter clubs, with higher lofts, should make a naturally descending blow into the ball. This helps to ensure the ball is struck before the ground making a crisp strike more likely. Your shorter clubs also have sufficient *loft* to elevate the ball without you having to manufacture any 'lifting' action of your own. As the clubs get longer and the loft decreases, the ball should be moved gradually forward (towards the target) within your stance ... your stance should also get gradually wider to accommodate the bigger, faster-moving clubs. The angle of approach into impact with the ball will, therefore, become shallower for each club as the ball is moved further forward until we get to the driver position … the ideal angle of approach for the driver being slightly upward through impact (it should be noted, however, that this upward angle of approach is merely a consequence of the forward ball position and not an intentionally altered swing).

Check your ball positions regularly as it is common for them to move, ever so slightly, out of place over time. A mispositioned ball in front of you could easily lead to a misdirected shot for no other reason.

13.7 Set Composition

This section refers to the mix of clubs that you should put in your bag and is relevant to the level of golf you are currently playing … or soon aspire to. If you put every type of club that is currently available on the market in your bag you would be 'lugging' about 25 clubs around with you … and we're only allowed to carry fourteen! In theory, you could carry about five wedges, nine irons, two or three hybrids, two or three fairway woods, a driver and a putter … but the rules don't allow this so you have to be selective.

Whatever the exact make-up of your set might be, it is important to know why each club is in your set and what it's there to achieve. In the early days, you may find that many of your irons go the same or similar distances to each other and, maybe, there is little point in carrying a full set. Buying just a half-set, or taking every other club out of your full set, will make deciding which club to play much more straightforward and obvious. For instance, if you don't know the distance gap between your seven and eight-iron they don't both need to be in your bag. A set comprising approximately three or four irons, one or two lofted hybrid/fairway woods and a putter, should be sufficient ... do not be tempted by a driver at this stage as it will get you into more trouble than it's worth.

However, as you gain experience and your ball-striking improves, you may well discover that there becomes a noticeable distance gap between the clubs in the half-set you started with. As long as you are sure that this gap is due to the gaps in your set (rather than the inconsistency in your ball-striking), then go ahead and fill the gaps with the appropriate clubs. Although, unless there is a consistent distance gap of at least ten yards between each club, there really isn't a gap to worry about at all.

Your next step, after your first half set, is to acquire a full set of irons ... although you shouldn't put any iron longer than a five or six-iron in the set at this stage. As the loft decreases and the length increases your clubs become much harder to strike cleanly and hit straight. You may now consider getting a full-size driver, but get one that has a reasonable amount of loft on it (around 12 degrees or more) and one that isn't too long (44 inches for men and 43 for ladies). Many 'off-the-shelf' drivers now have a length of up to 46 inches, but this is very uncontrollable - 44 inches should be the maximum for most people and, indeed, is the average on the professional tours around the world. You could then fill the gap between your driver and your longest iron with an 18–20-degree fairway wood and/or one or two hybrid/utility clubs in the loft range 20-28 degrees.

When acquiring hybrid clubs and fairway woods do not be fooled by the big number stamped on the bottom (3, 4, 5, 6, etc.); these numbers are only a guide and they vary greatly anyway from one manufacturer to another. The loft and length of a club are the principal things that make a club what it is. I have seen the sets of many players over the years and to see a number of conflicting clubs in the bag is quite common. The big numbers stamped on the club-head are, generally, logical but to see lower numbered clubs shorter than higher numbered clubs is not unusual. As a guide, if there isn't at least ½ an inch difference in length and three degrees difference in loft as the clubs get progressively longer from your pitching wedge to your driver, then you will not experience the correct performance difference between them.

As you progress even further, or are already playing off a single-figure handicap, you will become more attuned to the clubs you require in your bag. You will know more accurately how far each of your clubs will hit the ball (within a few yards at least, assuming they are struck cleanly) and you will know the types of clubs you prefer to play certain shots around the course ... especially your own course. You may be able to add longer irons into your set and reduce your distance gaps between clubs even further. You will also want to carry at least one extra wedge in addition to your pitching-wedge and sand-wedge, or even carry four different wedges as long as you feel they all do a different job.

A final word, in this section, on putters. Putters range in price from 'next-to-nothing' to the price of a small second-hand car, but they will all do the same job if the player holding onto it is proficient in their role. Some putters will be heavier or lighter and one type or another will feel just right to you. Some have bigger heads will alignment aids built into them and some may have very simple blade-shaped club-heads. The most important thing about your putter is that it feels right to YOU and is the right length to allow you to be in an ideal position to stroke the ball consistently (see chapter 8). Most 'off-the-shelf' putters are too long for the majority of people so you should have yours checked by a club-fitting professional.

Chapter 14

Concluding Thoughts

I sincerely hope you have enjoyed reading this book as much as I have enjoyed writing it? I have endeavoured to keep its contents as uncomplicated as possible and yet, where I feel it's important, give you the necessary technical information to help you understand what's important for your development; both, as a golfer and as a ball-striker.

I have not set out to fix your faults as other books, videos and articles tend to do, but to ask that you practice only the good habits that all better golfers display. Rather than focus on your bad habits (your faults) this book has set out to promote only the good habits which, if adopted by you, will automatically override and fix the majority of swing-faults.

I hope I have stressed sufficiently the importance of the grip and how a poor grip will severely hamper your performance and potential. A good grip will allow your swing to evolve in a naturally efficient and powerful way and also help you to control your clubface angle which is vital for accuracy.

Not only did I set out to help you understand and improve your swing, but also to give you a better understanding of the equipment you use, the obstacles you will encounter on the golf course, and how the weather may affect you. I have also touched on how your mind can disrupt your performance as much as your swing, but also given you some insights into how you can overcome your fears and anxieties.

You will also have noticed (I hope) how much of this book is devoted to your short-game and putting and learnt how influential these aspects of the game are to your score ... there is so much more to this game than thrashing a little white ball down a fairway!

My sincerest wish is that you have understood my teachings and philosophies, as laid out within these pages, and that they have helped you to improve your game. However, if there is any aspect or notion that you have not fully understood I would be only too happy to answer any questions that this book may evoke. My overriding ambition being to help everyone ... BECOME A BETTER GOLFER!

Enjoy this wonderful game,
Richard

(Contact information inside front cover)

Acknowledgements

It would not have been possible to publish my first golf book without the help, support, inspiration and patience of so many people. I have already thanked my family but I would like to acknowledge the support of the following friends and associates who have helped me complete this manuscript and send them my sincerest thanks.

To Stuart Sawyer. My friend and business partner from whom I have learnt so much over recent years ... mostly about people and how to get their best out of themselves.

To David Dibb. One of my first clients and now a close friend who, as a retired head-teacher, kindly proofread my first drafts and, consequently, has now officially become my new 'head of punctuation!

To Alan Piper. One of our most stalwart members who always donates time to help many others and kindly gave me his time to take the photographs you see in the book ... cheers Al, you're a star ... there are a few lessons in the bank for you!

To Annalisa. Long-suffering listener to my theories and ideas for this book ... she hasn't got a clue what I'm on about, bless her, but she's read the book (well, the cover at least) and said 'well-done love' at every juncture!

And finally, to Peter Palmer. As the reader of virtually every golf instruction book that's ever been written, Pete's opinion is the one I will cherish more than any. I'm sorry you're unwell at the moment Pete, but the first copy is for you!

About the Author

PGA Professional Richard Coffin has been playing and coaching golf for over 40 years. Now resident teaching

professional at The Westcountry Golf Academy near Tiverton, in Devon, Richard has finally chronicled the philosophies which have been at the core of his teaching for many years.

Starting at a tender age, tagging along behind his Father, Richard acquired an early passion for the game. Then, one-day a few years later, his parents came home and rather excitedly announced to their sixteen-year-old son that they had found him his dream job as 'trainee golf professional' at the local club. Although this didn't work out at the time, golf remained in his blood and a career in the golf equipment industry ensued (hence his other passion for custom-fitting and equipment technology). However, the desire to coach and help others improve their golf was still strong, and in 2009 Richard became one of the oldest Professional Golf Association (PGA) trainees in the UK and 3 years later graduated as a fully qualified PGA Professional.

It was this (unexpectedly academic) qualification that awakened Richard to the joys of writing and the power of the written word. Combine this with his varied and profound experiences within the sport and Richard, no doubt, offers a unique insight into helping people become better golfers.

31326950R00119

Printed in Poland
by Amazon Fulfillment
Poland Sp. z o.o., Wrocław